Copycat Recipes Cookbook

Thai Cuisine 100+ Tasty Recipes. The Complete Step-By-Step Guide to Cooking Delicious Dishes, from Appetizers to Desserts

Arsenio Islas

conjunction with this work. The Publisher acknowledges that the reader acts of their own accord and releases the author and Publisher of any responsibility for the observance of tips, advice, counsel, strategies and techniques that may be offered in this volume.

Tablet of contents

Chapter 4: Vegetable Recipes

Spaghetti Squash Pad Thai
Thai Pumpkin Curry
Thai Coconut Curry
Battered Veggies With Thai Sauce
Thai-Style Spicy Grilled Vegetable Skewers
One-Pot Red Curry
Thai Vegetable Chowder
Pad Pak Boong (Stir-Fried Morning Glory)
Pad Phuk Tong
Eggplant Green Curry

Chapter 5: Seafood Recipes

Thai Fish Cakes
Spicy Pepper and Garlic Shrimp
Thai-Style Crab Rice
Thai-Style Shrimp Burger
Thai Basil Rolls With Peanut and Hoisin Sauce
Steamed Mussels
Thai Tilapia
Thai Shrimp
Shrimp Pad Thai
Shrimp Red Curry
Thai Monkfish Curry
Grilled Prawns and Spicy Lime-Peanut
Vinaigrette
Steamed Crab Leg With Lemongrass
Grilled Mahi Mahi With Thai Coconut Sauce
Thai-Style Green Curry Prawns
Thai Fried Prawns With White Pepper and Garlic
Thai Clam and Shrimp Curry
Whole Fried Tilapia With Chilies and Basil

Chapter 6: Soupand Salad Recipes

Chapter 7: Tofu Recipes

Chapter 8: Snacks & Dessert Recipes

Conclusion

Introduction

Congratulations on purchasing *Thai Cuisine,* and thank you for doing so.

Every individual in this world loves to try out new flavors from different parts of the world every once in a while. However, due to certain circumstances, everyone can't travel the world to taste new cuisines. Wouldn't it be great if you could taste new flavors without any need to travel? In this book, you will come to know about Thai cuisine along with its specialties. I have included a wide array of recipes for you in this book to help you prepare the authentic dishes from Thailand right in your home kitchen. Thai cuisine is mostly about rice and noodles. With the help of this book, you will come to learn about many authentic dishes from Thailand apart from noodles and rice.

The first chapter is dedicated to the basics of Thai cuisine that will help you to learn about authentic Thai cuisine in general. Every part of Thailand has something special to offer. In this book, you will find a comprehensive approach to cook Thai dishes at home. The recipes are quite simple, and with minimal effort from your side, you can taste the actual essence of Thai cuisine.

There are plenty of books on this subject on the market, thanks again for choosing this one! Every effort was made to ensure it is full of as much useful information as possible, and please enjoy it!

Thanks again for choosing this book, make sure to leave a short review if you enjoy it, I'd really love to hear your thoughts.

Chapter 1: A Brief Introduction to Thai Cuisine

Food forms an integral part of any kind of social occasion in Thailand. A very interesting thing about Thai cuisine is that the food tends to become a reason for celebration or an occasion in itself. The main reason behind this is the social and friendly nature of the people of Thailand. Also, the way in which Thai cuisine is eaten and ordered is in itself unique. Any typical Thai meal will consist of four types of seasonings – salt, spicy, sour, and sweet. Most of the dishes from Thailand are not considered to be satisfying until all the tastes of these four seasonings are combined. A traditional Thai dining experience would include a wide variety of fish or meat dishes, some veggies, a simple dish of noodles, and a soup. The desserts might have simple and fresh fruits like pineapple or something exotic and colorful like rice cakes. It will all depend on which region you are in.

Besides the simple and elegant cuisines of Thailand, people over there are great smackers as well. Some of the most popular Thai snacks include beef or chicken satay, spring rolls, egg rolls, crepes, and raw fresh veggies with a dipping sauce. Additionally, the presentation of Thai food is something that you should experience. Thai cuisine presentation falls under the category of most exquisite presentations in the whole world. The serving platters are generally decorated with carved fruits and vegetables into flowers along with other beautiful shapes. The stir-fries that are palace-style are considered as a piece of art.

The modern-day taste of Thai dishes has a great influence from the country's ancient history. The people of Thailand established the heart of Siamese cuisine with various types of seafood and meat combined with herbs, vegetables, and spices. Noodles were brought to Thailand by the Chinese, and the most important cooking tool of Thailand – steel wok. It has been found that Thai cuisine comes with great influence from the Indian flavors and spices as well. However, Thai dishes come with a distinct characteristic that helps differentiate them from the Indian dishes and curries. This point of differentiation is the use of lemongrass, holy basil, and Thai ginger or galangal.

Thai cuisine is known for its colorful curries and the super spicy experience that you are going to have. There are four specific types of colors in Thai curries that can be found – red, green, orange, and yellow. Also, the cuisine can be differentiated based on the various regions. For example, Thai cuisine in the northern region of Thailand is simple in comparison to the other regions where sticky rice is always preferred. The central region of Thailand is all about royal cuisines. On the other hand, the southern region of Thailand involves coconut milk and coconut oil for cooking. So, it is evident that each region comes with a specific characteristic of its own.

I have included a wide array of Thai recipes from various regions in the next chapters.

Chapter 2: Rice And Noodles Recipes

Thai cuisine is based mainly on rice and noodles. No matter what kind of dish you order in a Thai restaurant, noodles, or rice is a must-have with any dish. In this chapter, I have included some of the most famous rice and noodles recipes from Thailand that you can easily make at your home.

Thai Pineapple Fried Rice

Total Prep & Cooking Time: Forty minutes
Yields: Six servings
Nutrition Facts: Calories: 621 | Protein: 17g | Carbs: 122g | Fat: 5.9g | Fiber: 7.2g

Ingredients

- Three tbsps. of oil
- Four cups of rice (cooked)
- Two tbsps. of soy sauce
- Two tsps. of curry powder
- Two shallots (chopped)
- Three garlic cloves (chopped)
- One green or red chili (sliced)
- One-fourth cup of vegetable broth
- One large egg
- One can of pineapple chunks (drained)
- Half cup of raisins
- One-third cup of whole cashews (unsalted, roasted)

- Three scallions (sliced)
- Three-fourth cup of cilantro

Method:

1. Start by mixing one tbsp. of oil with the cooked rice. Separate any big chunks using your fingers. Keep aside.

2. Stir the curry powder and soy sauce in a small cup.

3. Add two tbsps. Of oil in a frying pan. Add garlic, shallots, along with the chili. Stir-fry the mixture for about one minute.

4. You can add one tbsp of vegetable broth for keeping all the ingredients sizzling.

5. Crack the egg into the mixture. Scramble the egg with the vegetables.

6. Add the remaining veggies and stir well.

7. Add pineapple chunks, rice, cashews, and raisins.

8. Add the mixture of curry powder and soy sauce over the rice and combine well. Stir-fry for two minutes.

9. In case the ingredients are dry, you can add one tbsp. of oil from the sides.

10. Season the rice with pepper and salt.

11. Serve the pineapple fried rice with cilantro and scallions from the top.

Thai Chicken Rice

Total Prep & Cooking Time: Thirty minutes
Yields: Four servings
Nutrition Facts: Calories: 720 | Protein: 38g | Carbs:
129g | Fat: 20.3g | Fiber: 2.2g

Ingredients

- Five cups of rice (cooked)
- One breast of chicken (chopped in small bits)
- One tbsp. of soy sauce
- Three tbsps. of vegetable oil
- Four spring onions (sliced)
- Four garlic cloves (minced)
- One green or red chili (sliced)
- Seven shitake mushrooms (chopped)
- One celery stalk (sliced)
- Two tbsps. of chicken stock
- Half cup of peas (frozen)
- One large egg

For the sauce:

- Three tbsps. of each
- Fish sauce
- Chicken broth
- Two tbsps. of soy sauce
- One tbsp. of lime juice
- One-third tsp. of white pepper
- One tsp. of sugar

Method:

1. Use some oil for separating the large chunks of rice with the help of your fingers.

2. Add the chicken in a medium-sized bowl. Add the soy sauce and mix well. Keep aside.

3. Combine all the listed ingredients for the sauce in a small cup. Mix well.

4. Heat a large wok and drizzle two tbsps. Of oil in it. Start adding the spring onions along with the chili and garlic.

5. Stir-fry the mixture for one minute. Start adding the marinated chicken and cook for three minutes until browned.

6. Add the shitake mushrooms along with the celery. Fry the mixture for three minutes. In case the wok gets dry, add two tbsps. of oil along with some broth and keep cooking.

7. Add the cooked rice and mix well using a spatula.

8. Add the sauce, two tbsps. at one time. Stir-fry the mixture for six minutes.

9. Add the peas and mix well.

10. Make a well at the center. Crack in the egg. Scramble the egg.

11. Mix all the ingredients together over high heat for two minutes.

12. Serve hot.

Thai Shrimp Fried Rice

Total Prep & Cooking Time: Thirty minutes
Yields: Two servings
Nutrition Facts: Calories: 383 | Protein: 2.3g | Carbs: 21.9g | Fat: 25.7g | Fiber: 1.2g

Ingredients

- Four cups of rice (cooked)
- Twelve shrimps
- Four tbsps. of cooking white wine
- One-fourth cup of onion (chopped)
- Four cloves of garlic (minced)
- Two large eggs
- Three-fourth cup of peas

For the sauce:

- Half tsp. of shrimp paste
- Two tbsps. of fish sauce
- Three tbsps. of soy sauce
- One tsp. of sugar
- One pinch of white pepper
- Two tsps. of chili sauce
- One green onion (sliced, for garnishing)

Method:

1. Mix all the listed ingredients for the sauce in a cup. Keep aside.

2. Heat a wok. Drizzle two tbsps. of oil in the wok. Add the onions along with the garlic. Fry the ingredients for one minute.

3. Add the cooking white wine and stir-fry for two minutes.

4. Start adding the shrimps. Cook for three minutes until the shrimps change color to pink.

5. Push the cooked shrimps to one side and add one tsp. of oil in the wok. Crack the eggs and scramble for one minute.

6. Now it is time to add the rice along with the peas. Mix well. Add the prepared sauce over the rice and toss.

7. Stir-fry the rice by tossing for four minutes.

8. Serve the shrimp rice with green onions from the top.

Spicy Chicken and Basil Fried Rice

Total Prep & Cooking Time: Forty minutes
Yields: Six servings
Nutrition Facts: Calories: 792 | Protein: 27.2g | Carbs: 114.6g | Fat: 23.2g | Fiber: 3.6g

Ingredients

- Three tbsps. of oyster sauce
- One tsp. of white sugar
- Two tbsps. of fish sauce
- Half cup of peanut oil
- Four cups of jasmine rice (cooked)
- Six garlic cloves (crushed)
- Two Serrano peppers (crushed)
- One pound of chicken breast (cut in thin strips)
- One large red pepper (sliced thinly)
- One onion (sliced)
- Two cups of Thai basil
- One cucumber (sliced)
- Half cup sprigs of cilantro

Method:

1. Combine fish sauce, oyster sauce, and white sugar in a small bowl. Keep aside.

2. Heat oil in a wok over a medium flame. Start adding the Serrano pepper and garlic. Cook for one minute.

3. Add the strips of chicken, onion, mixture of oyster sauce, and pepper. Keep cooking until the chicken strips are tender.

4. Start adding the cooked rice along with the basil leaves and combine them. Keep mixing until the sauce mixes with the rice properly.

5. Serve with cilantro, cucumber slices, and basil leaves.

Khao NeeoMamuang (Sweet Sticky Rice and Mango)

Total Prep & Cooking Time: One hour and forty minutes
Yields: Four servings
Nutrition Facts: Calories: 810 | Protein: 8.2g | Carbs: 134.6g | Fat: 23.7g | Fiber: 7.2g

Ingredients

- Two cups of white rice (short-grain, uncooked)
- Two and a half cup of water
- One and a half cup of coconut milk
- One cup of white sugar
- One-fourth tsp. of salt
- One tbsp. of tapioca starch
- Three mangoes (sliced)
- One-third tsp. of sesame seeds (toasted)

Method:

1. Mix water and rice in a large pan. Boil the mixture and simmer for twenty minutes until all the water is absorbed.

2. While the rice is cooking, combine one cup of coconut milk, salt, and sugar in a pan over a medium flame. Boil the mixture. Remove the pan from the heat. Keep aside.

3. Add the cooked rice in the mixture of coconut milk. Cool the mixture for one hour.

4. Mix the remaining coconut milk along with salt, tapioca starch, and sugar in a pan. Boil the mixture.

5. Arrange the sticky rice on serving plates. Add the sliced mangoes from the top. Pour the prepared sauce over the rice and mangoes. Serve with sesame seeds from the top.

Thai Yellow Rice With Veggies

Total Prep & Cooking Time: One hour and thirty minutes
Yields: Four servings
Nutrition Facts: Calories: 418 | Protein: 11.6g | Carbs: 74.6g | Fat: 7.4g | Fiber: 4.9g

Ingredients

- Two tbsps. of vegetable oil
- One-fourth cup of onion (chopped)
- Three garlic cloves (minced)
- One-eighth tsp. of chili flakes
- One-fourth cup of red pepper (diced)
- One tomato (diced)
- Two cups of Thai jasmine rice (uncooked)
- Four cups of chicken broth
- One lime (juiced)
- Two tbsps. of fish sauce
- Half tsp. of turmeric
- One-third tsp. of saffron
- Half cup of peas (frozen)
- Salt
- A handful of basil (for garnishing)

Method:

1. Take a deep pot and heat it over a medium flame. Drizzle some oil in the pot. Start adding the garlic, onion, and chili. Keep cooking for one minute.

2. Add the tomato and red pepper. Stir-fry the ingredients for one minute.

3. Add the jasmine rice and mix well for coating. Add the stock and turn the flame to high.

4. Add fish sauce, lime juice, saffron, and turmeric. Mix well. Boil the mixture and cover the pot with a lid. Cook the rice for twenty minutes until all the liquid gets absorbed.

5. Open the lid and add the peas. Mix again.

6. Cook for ten minutes.

7. Serve with basil from the top.

Thai Beef Rice

Total Prep & Cooking Time: Thirty minutes
Yields: Four servings
Nutrition Facts: Calories: 707 | Protein: 42g | Carbs: 50.3g | Fat: 34.6g | Fiber: 2.9g

Ingredients

- One tbsp. of vegetable oil
- Half tsp. of sesame oil
- Half cup of red bell pepper (diced)
- One-fourth cup of onion (diced)
- One green onion (chopped)
- One-third tsp. of garlic powder
- Half pound of ground beef (cooked, crumbled)
- One-third cup of fresh tomato (diced)
- Two tbsps. of each
- Soy sauce
- Fish sauce
- Two cups of jasmine rice (cooked)
- One tsp. of each
- Black pepper (ground)
- Salt
- Two lime wedges
- One large egg (beaten)

Method:

1. Take a wok and warm some vegetable oil in it. Add the vegetables and keep cooking for two minutes. Add the ground beef and mix well.

Sprinkle some garlic powder from the top and cook the mixture for one minute.

2. Add the fish sauce, diced tomatoes, and soy sauce. Sauté the mixture for two minutes. Add the cooked rice and combine well. Add pepper, salt, and squeeze the wedges of lime.

3. Cook the beaten egg in another pan. Cook for two minutes and flip. Fold the egg in half and keep aside.

4. Serve the prepared rice in serving plates and top with half omelet for each plate.

Mushroom Fried Rice

Total Prep & Cooking Time: Thirty minutes
Yields: Two servings
Nutrition Facts: Calories: 320 | Protein: 8.9g | Carbs: 46.2g | Fat: 14.9g | Fiber: 7.6g

Ingredients

- Five cups of cooked rice
- One tbsp. of mirin
- One shallot (chopped)
- One red chili (minced)
- Six mushrooms (sliced)
- One-third stalk of celery (sliced)
- Half of a yellow bell pepper (sliced)
- One-fourth cup of frozen peas
- One large egg
- Handful of coriander
- Two tbsps. of vegetable oil

For the sauce:

- Four tbsps. of vegetable stock
- Two tbsps. of soy sauce
- Half tsp. of brown sugar
- One tbsp. of hoisin sauce

Method:

1. Mix all the listed ingredients for the sauce in a bowl. Keep aside.

2. Drizzle some oil in a wok and add the chopped shallots. Cook for one minute and add the mushrooms along with the chili. Add some mirin for keeping the pan moist.

3. Add the bell pepper along with the celery. Start adding the rice along with the sauce. Cook for one minute.

4. Make a well in the center. Crack the egg. Scramble the egg and toss it with the rice.

5. Cook the rice for one minute.

6. Serve with coriander from the top.

Thai Coconut Rice

Total Prep & Cooking Time: One hour
Yields: Four servings
Nutrition Facts: Calories: 429 | Protein: 11.3g | Carbs: 80.1g | Fat: 12.7g | Fiber: 12.6g

Ingredients

- Two cups of white jasmine rice
- One can of coconut milk
- Three tbsps. of shredded coconut
- Salt
- One and a half cup of water
- Half tsp. of coconut oil

Method:

1. Add the rice to a large deep pot and add the coconut milk. Add half a cup of water along with shredded coconut. Add some salt and stir for mixing.

2. Boil the mixture and cover the pot. Simmer for twenty minutes.

3. Open the lid and check if any liquid exists. If there is still some liquid left, cover the pot and simmer for five minutes.

4. Turn off the heat. Let the rice sit for five minutes.

5. Use a fork for fluffing the rice

6. Serve the rice warm with a little bit of shredded coconut from the top.

Pad Thai Noodles

Total Prep & Cooking Time: One hour
Yields: Four servings
Nutrition Facts: Calories: 531.2 | Protein: 34.3g |
Carbs: 64.6g | Fat: 14.7g | Fiber: 3.2g

Ingredients

- Seven ounces of thick rice noodles
- Two tbsps. of each
- Peanuts
- Vegetable oil
- Six Thai peppers (minced)
- One shallot (minced)
- Three garlic cloves (minced)
- One pound breast of chicken (cut in strips of half an inch)
- One-third cup of tofu (extra firm, cut in matchsticks)
- Three tbsps. of white sugar
- Two and a half tbsp. of tamarind paste
- One and a half tbsp. of fish sauce
- Half tsp. of white pepper (ground)
- One large egg
- One-fourth pound of large shrimp
- One cup of each
- Chives (chopped)
- Bean sprouts
- One lime (juiced)

Method:

1. Add the noodles in a deep pot and use hot water for covering the same. Let the noodles sit for ten minutes until firm. Drain the water.

2. Take a wok and heat one tbsp. of oil in it. Add the peanuts and cook them for two minutes. Keep aside.

3. Add the shallot, peppers, and garlic into the wok. Stir-fry for thirty seconds. Add the tofu and chicken. Keep cooking for five minutes. Add the soaked noodles and toss well.

4. Add tamarind paste, sugar, white pepper, and fish sauce. Stir well for combining and cook for two minutes.

5. Push the cooked noodles to a side and crack the egg in the center of the wok. Scramble the egg and combine it properly with the noodles. Add the shrimp and stir-fry for three minutes.

6. Add bean sprouts, peanuts, lime juice, and chives. Mix well.

7. Serve with peanuts from the top.

**Rice Noodle Salad**

Total Prep & Cooking Time: Thirty minutes
Yields: Four servings
Nutrition Facts: Calories: 470.2 | Protein: 3.6g |
Carbs: 64.6g | Fat: 20.9g | Fiber: 2.6g

Ingredients

- Eight ounces of rice noodles
- One tbsp. of olive oil
- One-fourth head of romaine lettuce (chopped)
- One-fourth red bell pepper (diced)
- One-fourth cup of red onion (chopped)
- Three green onions (chopped)
- One-fourth cucumber (diced)
- Two tbsps. of each
- Basil (chopped)
- Cilantro (chopped)
- One inch piece of ginger (minced)
- One-fourth of jalapeno pepper (minced)
- Two garlic cloves (minced)

For the sauce:

- One-third cup of olive oil
- One-fourth cup of each
- Rice vinegar
- White sugar
- Soy sauce
- One lemon (juiced)
- One tsp. of salt

- One-fourth tsp. of each
- Paprika
- Turmeric (ground)

Method:

1. Take a bowl of water. Soak the rice noodles. Let the noodles soak for ten minutes until softened. Drain the water and add one tbsp of olive oil. Toss for coating.

2. Combine red bell pepper, lettuce, red onion, basil, green onions, cilantro, cucumber, jalapeno pepper, ginger, and minced garlic with the noodles.

3. Mix the listed ingredients for the sauce in a medium-sized bowl.

4. Pour the sauce over the noodle salad and toss for combining.

One-Pot Rice Noodles

Total Prep & Cooking Time: Forty minutes
Yields: Four servings
Nutrition Facts: Calories: 576.2 | Protein: 15.4g |
Carbs: 96.4g | Fat: 9.1g | Fiber: 3.7g

Ingredients

- Two tbsps. of cornstarch
- One and a half tbsp. of water
- Six cups of chicken stock
- Three tbsps. of soy sauce
- One tbsp. of fish sauce
- Half tbsp. of rice vinegar
- One-third tbsp. of chili-garlic sauce
- Two tsps. of each
- Garlic (minced)
- Vegetable oil
- Ginger (minced)
- One tsp. of coriander (ground)
- Sixteen ounces of rice noodles
- One cup of each
- Red bell pepper (sliced)
- Zucchini (sliced)
- Two breasts of chicken (cooked, cut in small cubes)
- Half cup of each
- Cilantro (chopped)
- Peanuts (crushed)

Method:

1. Combine the cornstarch along with some water in a cup. Combine the mixture of cornstarch with chicken stock, fish sauce, soy sauce, chili-garlic sauce, rice vinegar, garlic, ginger, vegetable oil, and coriander. Boil the mixture.

2. Add the rice noodles in the sauce and simmer for ten minutes until the noodles are tender. Add red bell pepper, zucchini, and cubes of chicken. Boil the mixture and simmer for five minutes.

3. Serve with cilantro and peanuts from the top.

Thai Pesto Noodles

Total Prep & Cooking Time: Twenty minutes
Yields: Four servings
Nutrition Facts: Calories: 112 | Protein: 5.9g | Carbs: 8.9g | Fat: 9.8g | Fiber: 1.6g

Ingredients

- Ten ounces of rice noodles (thick)
- One bunch of cilantro
- One-fourth cup of peanut butter
- Three garlic cloves (minced)
- Three tbsps. of olive oil (extra virgin)
- Two tbsps. of ginger (minced)
- One and a half tbsp. of fish sauce
- One tbsp. of brown sugar
- Half tsp. of cayenne pepper

Method:

1. Soak the rice noodles in warm water. Soak them for about ten minutes. Let the noodles sit until tender.

2. In the meantime, combine peanut butter, olive oil, garlic, ginger, brown sugar, fish sauce, and pepper in a food processor. Keep blending until smooth.

3. Heat some oil in a wok. Add the pesto sauce. Cook for one minute. Add the soaked noodles

and toss them for combining. Cook for one minute.

4. Serve hot.

Thai Noodle Curry Bowl

Total Prep & Cooking Time: Thirty minutes
Yields: Six servings
Nutrition Facts: Calories: 208.3 | Protein: 3.4g |
Carbs: 37.2g | Fat: 4.7g | Fiber: 1.7g

Ingredients

- One tbsp. of peanut oil
- Two garlic cloves (minced)
- Thirty ounces of Thai ginger broth
- One carrot (cut in matchsticks)
- Eight ounces of rice noodles (thick, cooked)
- Three tbsps. of green onions (sliced)
- One-third cup of cilantro (chopped)
- Two tbsps. of peanuts (chopped)
- Six lime wedges

Method:

1. Heat some oil in a pot. Add the garlic. Stir-fry for thirty seconds.

2. Add the ginger broth and boil. Add the sliced carrots and cook them for five minutes.

3. Add the cooked noodles and simmer for four minutes.

4. Serve the curry noodles in serving bowls with cilantro, peanuts, and green onions from the top.

Pas See Ew (Noodles With Broccoli and Beef)

Total Prep & Cooking Time: Thirty-five minutes
Yields: Eight servings
Nutrition Facts: Calories: 182.3 | Protein: 5.7g |
Carbs: 24.7g | Fat: 5.9g | Fiber: 0.9g

Ingredients

- Eight ounces of thick rice noodles
- One cup of broccoli (cut in bite-size pieces)
- One tbsp. of vegetable oil
- One tsp. of garlic (crushed)
- Half pound of rib-eye steak (thinly sliced)
- Half cup of water
- One and a half tbsp. of cornstarch
- Three tbsps. of each
- Soy sauce
- Oyster sauce
- Two tbsps. of each
- White sugar
- Fish sauce
- Half tsp. of each
- Black pepper (ground)
- Salt
- One large egg

Method:

1. Place the noodles in a large bowl. Cover it using hot water. Soak the noodles for ten minutes. Drain the water and keep aside.

2. Boil water in a small pot. Add the pieces of broccoli and cook for seven minutes until firm. Drain the water and keep aside.

3. Heat the oil in a large skillet. Add the garlic. Cook for three minutes and add the steak. Cook for seven minutes until the meat pieces are tender.

4. Combine the cornstarch along with some water in a bowl. Add the mixture to the skillet. Add soy sauce, oyster sauce, sugar, and fish sauce. Stir the mixture.

5. Add the broccoli along with the noodles. Add pepper and salt for seasoning.

6. Cook the egg in another skillet.

7. Add the cooked eggs to the noodles and mix well.

8. Serve hot.

Spicy Peanut Noodles

Total Prep & Cooking Time: Thirty-five minutes
Yields: Six servings
Nutrition Facts: Calories: 680.2 | Protein: 25.7g |
Carbs: 80.3g | Fat: 27.2g | Fiber: 5.7g

Ingredients

For the sauce:

- Half cup of peanut butter
- Six tbsps. of soy sauce
- Three tbsps. of each
- Rice vinegar
- Brown sugar
- Sesame oil
- Two red chilies (chopped)
- Two tbsps. of each
- Ginger (grated)
- Chili-garlic sauce
- One tsp. of fish sauce
- Half tsp. of black pepper (ground)

For the noodles:

- Three tbsps. of olive oil
- One pound of chicken breast (cut in cubes of three-fourth inch)
- One cup of carrots (cut in matchsticks)
- One red bell pepper (sliced in strips)
- Four green onions (sliced)

- Two cups of bean sprouts (rinsed)
- One-fourth cup of cilantro (chopped)
- Sixteen ounces of rice noodles
- One tbsp. of peanuts (chopped)

Method:

1. Whisk all the listed ingredients for the sauce in a bowl. Keep aside.

2. Take a large wok and heat two tbsps. of oil in it. Add the pieces of chicken and cook for three minutes. Add one-fourth cup of the sauce to the chicken. Cook for two minutes. Transfer the cooked chicken along with the juices in a bowl.

3. Heat the leftover oil and add the carrots. Cook for three minutes and add the bell peppers. Cook for one minute. Add the chicken, green onions, remaining sauce, cilantro, and bean sprouts. Cook the mixture for one minute.

4. Cover the noodles with hot water for five minutes. Drain the water and add the cooked noodles to the mixture.

5. Add the peanuts and stir-fry for two minutes.

6. Serve the noodles with peanuts from the top.

Pad Kee Mao (Thai Drunken Noodles)

Total Prep & Cooking Time: Thirty-five minutes
Yields: Four servings
Nutrition Facts: Calories: 567.3 | Protein: 7.3g |
Carbs: 106.3g | Fat: 12.2g | Fiber: 4.6g

Ingredients

- One pound of rice noodles (dried)
- Three tbsps. of oil
- One-fourth cup of each
- Thai chilies
- Onion (sliced)
- Two tbsps. of each
- Garlic (minced)
- Soy sauce
- Fish sauce
- One tbsp. of brown sugar
- One red bell pepper (cut in pieces of one inch)
- One cup of each
- Peapods
- Broccoli (chopped)
- Half cup of carrots (chopped)
- One-third cup of basil (chopped)

Method:

1. Add the noodles in a pot and cover with hot water. Add one tbsp. of oil to the noodles and soak for ten minutes. Drain the water and keep aside.

2. Take a large wok and heat the oil in it. Add the onion, chilies, and garlic. Fry the mixture for five minutes. Add the fish sauce, brown sugar, and soy sauce. Stir the mixture. Add the noodles, broccoli, bell pepper, carrots, and pea pods. Stir-fry the mixture for five minutes. Add the basil.

3. Serve the noodles with basil from the top.

Thai Noodle Pork Bowl

Total Prep & Cooking Time: Thirty minutes
Yields: Six servings
Nutrition Facts: Calories: 590.3 | Protein: 21.5g |
Carbs: 44.6g | Fat: 36.5g | Fiber: 4.9g

Ingredients

- Twelve ounces of rice noodles (wide)
- One-fourth cup of soy sauce
- One tbsp. of each
- Vegetable oil
- Honey
- Ginger paste
- Garlic (chopped)
- Two tsps. of fish sauce
- Two tbsps. of red curry paste
- One can of coconut milk
- Two pounds of pork loin chops (cut in thin strips)
- One cup of carrots (julienned)
- Eight ounces of sugar snap peas
- One-third cup of cilantro (chopped)
- Half lime (juiced and zested)

Method:

1. Boil water in a large pot. Add some oil. Add the noodles and cook for two minutes. Drain the water and keep aside.

2. Whisk honey, soy sauce, and fish sauce in a bowl.

3. Take an iron skillet and add some oil in it. Add the ginger paste, garlic, and curry paste. Cook for one minute. Add the coconut milk and cook for one minute.

4. Add the strips of pork, peas, and carrots. Cook for five minutes. Add the mixture of soy sauce. Simmer the mixture for five minutes. Add the noodles and stir for one minute.

5. Serve the noodles hot with lime zest, lime juice, and cilantro from the top.

Rad Na Noodles

Total Prep & Cooking Time: Thirty minutes
Yields: Four servings
Nutrition Facts: Calories: 310.3 | Protein: 12.6g |
Carbs: 35.9g | Fat: 13.6g | Fiber: 2.9g

Ingredients

- Two large eggs (beaten)
- Three tbsps. of each
- Fish sauce
- Soy sauce
- Brown sugar
- Rice vinegar
- One head of romaine lettuce
- Half tsp. of pepper flakes
- Six scallions (sliced)
- Half pound of bean sprouts
- One cup of peanuts (chopped)
- Eight ounces of rice noodles (wide)
- Two tbsps. of vegetable oil
- Hot sauce (for serving)

Method:

1. Start by cooking the noodles in hot water for five minutes. Drain the water and keep aside.

2. Whisk together fish sauce, soy sauce, rice vinegar, brown sugar, and three tbsps. of water in a bowl.

3. Slice the lettuce into pieces of half an inch. Heat some oil in a large wok. Add the pepper flakes. Add the noodles and coat in oil. Add the prepared sauce toss for one minute.

4. Cook the eggs as omelet in a skillet. Slice the omelet into thin slices.

5. Add the eggs, scallions, nuts, and bean sprouts to the noodles. Cook for one minute.

6. Serve hot with hot sauce from the top.

Creamy Thai Noodles

Total Prep & Cooking Time: Forty-five minutes
Yields: Four servings
Nutrition Facts: Calories: 336.3 | Protein: 12g | Carbs: 49.6g | Fat: 10.7g | Fiber: 4.9g

Ingredients

- Eight ounces of noodles
- One tbsp. of vegetable oil
- One tsp. of ginger (grated)
- Two garlic cloves (minced)
- Half cup of carrot (julienned)
- Two cups of cabbage (sliced)
- One-fourth cup of bean sprouts
- Cilantro, green onions, and peanuts (for garnishing)

For the sauce:

- Half cup of chicken stock
- Two tbsps. of each
- Soy sauce
- Peanut butter (creamy)
- One tsp. of sriracha
- Two tsps. of sesame oil
- One tbsp. of brown sugar
- One-fourth tsp. of red pepper flakes

Method:

1. Combine the listed ingredients for the sauce in a bowl. Keep aside.

2. Cook the noodles in boiling water for five minutes. Drain the water and keep aside.

3. Add oil in a wok and cook the garlic along with the ginger.

4. Add cabbage and carrots. Cook for three minutes. Add the prepared sauce and simmer for three minutes.

5. Add the noodles along with the bean sprouts. Toss well for two minutes.

6. Serve the noodles with cilantro, peanuts, and green onions from the top.

**Rainbow Veggie Pad Thai**

Total Prep & Cooking Time: Twenty minutes
Yields: Four servings
Nutrition Facts: Calories: 323.3 | Protein: 7.8g |
Carbs: 35.7g | Fat: 16.7g | Fiber: 3.7g

Ingredients

- Four ounces of brown rice noodles
- One zucchini
- One red bell pepper
- Two carrots
- Half an onion
- Two tbsps. of oil
- One large egg (beaten)
- Half cup of peanuts (chopped)
- One cup of fresh herbs (green onions, cilantro, and basil)

For the sauce:

- Three tbsps. of each
- Fish sauce
- Chicken stock
- Brown sugar
- Two tbsps. of white vinegar
- One tbsp. of soy sauce
- One tsp. of chili paste

Method:

1. Start by spiralizing the veggies using a spiralizer or a peeler. In case you do not have a peeler, you can cut them into thin strips.

2. Add the ingredients of the sauce in a bowl and combine.

3. Take a wok and heat some oil in it. Add the vegetables and cook for two minutes. Transfer the veggies to a bowl.

4. Cook the noodles in hot water for five minutes. Drain the water. Add the noodles to the wok.

5. Add the prepared sauce and toss the noodles. Push the noodles to one side and break the egg in the center. Scramble the egg. Combine it with the noodles.

6. Add the cooked vegetables to the wok and stir-fry for two minutes. Add the herbs.

7. Serve hot.

Thai Garlic and Ginger Noodle Bowl

Total Prep & Cooking Time: Forty-five minutes
Yields: Four servings
Nutrition Facts: Calories: 389.3 | Protein: 7.8g |
Carbs: 68.6g | Fat: 10.3g | Fiber: 9.3g

Ingredients

- Eight ounces of rice noodles
- Ten ounces of snow peas
- Two tbsps. of sesame oil
- Two tsps. of ginger (grated)
- One tbsp. of garlic (minced)
- Two cups of carrots (julienned)
- Five cups of cabbage (cut in bite-size pieces)
- Five ounces of shitake mushrooms (sliced in quarters, steamed)

For the sauce:

- Half cup of vegetable stock
- One tbsp. of sesame oil
- Two tbsps. of tamari
- Half tbsp. of coconut sugar
- One-third tsp. of each
- Sea salt
- Pepper flakes

Method:

1. Soak the noodles in hot water for about five minutes. Drain the water and keep aside.

2. Blanch the snow peas in a pot of water for two minutes. Trim the ends before blanching. Drain the water and keep aside.

3. Whisk the listed ingredients for the sauce in a small bowl. Keep aside.

4. Take a large wok and heat some oil in it. Add the garlic and ginger. Cook for thirty seconds and add the mushrooms. Cook for one minute. Add the carrots and cabbage. Cook for two minutes. Keep the veggies aside along with the peas.

5. Add the sauce in the wok and simmer for two minutes. Add the noodles and toss for coating.

6. Add the vegetable mix and stir for two minutes.

7. Serve the noodles hot.

Chapter 3: Meat and Poultry Recipes

Meat and poultry are important parts of any kind of cuisine. In this chapter, you will find various Thai recipes based on meat and poultry. Let's have a look at them.

Thai Broccoli and Beef Stir-Fry

Total Prep & Cooking Time: Thirty minutes
Yields: Four servings
Nutrition Facts: Calories: 460 | Protein: 30.2g | Carbs: 41.3g | Fat: 20.1g | Fiber: 6.9g

Ingredients

- One pound of beef steak
- Three tbsps. of vegetable oil
- One shallot (chopped)
- Four garlic cloves (chopped)
- Two pieces of ginger (sliced in matchsticks)
- Two tbsps. of red wine
- One small head of broccoli (cut the florets in bite-size pieces)
- One red pepper (sliced in strips)
- One tsp. of cornstarch (combine in three tbsps. of water)
- Half tsp. of sesame oil

For the marinade:

- Three tbsps. of soy sauce
- One tsp. of brown sugar
- Half tsp. of cornstarch

For the sauce:

- Half cup of chicken stock
- Three tbsps. of oyster sauce
- One tbsp. of fish sauce
- Two tsps. of brown sugar
- Two red chilies (minced)

Method:

1. Start by cutting the steak into long strips of two inches.

2. Combine the marinade ingredients in a bowl.

3. Pour the prepared marinade over the steak and combine it. Keep aside.

4. Combine the sauce ingredients in a bowl and keep aside.

5. Take a large wok and heat the oil in it. Add the shallots, ginger, and garlic. Cook for one minute. Add the marinated beef and cook for five minutes until browned.

6. Add the red wine for keeping the wok moist.

7. Add the red pepper along with the broccoli. Add the sauce. Lower the flame and cook for five minutes.

8. Add the mixture of cornstarch and combine.

9. Serve the dish with Thai jasmine rice by the side.

Thai Grilled Steak

Total Prep & Cooking Time: Two hours and thirty minutes
Yields: Two servings
Nutrition Facts: Calories: 331 | Protein: 21.3g | Carbs: 57.3g | Fat: 5.3g | Fiber: 6.9g

Ingredients

- Two beef steaks

For the marinade:

- Four cloves of garlic (minced)
- One-fourth cup of onion (chopped)
- Two chilies (minced)
- Three tbsps. of hoisin sauce
- Four tbsps. of soy sauce
- One tbsp. of fish sauce
- Half tsp. of lime juice
- Two tbsps. of brown sugar

Method:

1. Combine the marinade ingredients in a bowl. Mix well for dissolving the sugar.

2. Marinate the steaks with the prepared marinade. Cover the steaks and refrigerate for two hours.

3. Add the steaks to a hot grill pan. Cook for seven minutes on each side.

4. Slice the steaks in strips (if desired) and serve with the pan juice from the top.

Massaman Thai Beef Curry

Total Prep & Cooking Time: Two hours and ten minutes
Yields: Four servings
Nutrition Facts: Calories: 731 | Protein: 50.3g | Carbs: 44.6g | Fat: 38.9g | Fiber: 6.4g

Ingredients

- Two cups of beef stock
- Two pounds of beef (cut in cubes)
- One-third cup of onion (diced)
- Three bay leaves
- Two potatoes (cut in chunks)
- A handful of basil

For the sauce:

- One piece of ginger (grated)
- Five garlic cloves
- One lemongrass stalk (minced)
- One red chili (sliced)
- One-fourth cup of peanuts (chopped)
- One tsp. of each
- Cumin seed
- Coriander (ground)
- Turmeric
- Brown sugar
- Tamarind
- Half tsp. of white pepper
- One-eighth tsp. of cardamom

- Three-fourth tsp. of shrimp paste
- Two tbsps. of fish sauce
- One can of coconut milk

Method:

1. Start by adding the stock in a large pot. Add the onion, meat, along with the bay leaves. Add the lemongrass.

2. Boil the mixture and simmer for one hour by covering with a lid.

3. Add the ingredients for the sauce and stir well.

4. Add the potatoes and simmer for thirty minutes.

5. Serve the beef curry with basil from the top.

Thai Beef Coconut Curry

Total Prep & Cooking Time: One hour
Yields: Four servings
Nutrition Facts: Calories: 350 | Protein: 7.6g | Carbs:
19.3g | Fat: 37.3g | Fiber: 7.8g

Ingredients

- Two beef steaks (cut in thin slices)
- One can of coconut milk
- One small onion (sliced in rings)
- Two cups of pineapple chunks
- Half cup of cherry tomatoes
- Three tbsps. of oil
- One-fourth cup of beef stock
- Two tbsps. of red wine
- Two bay leaves
- A handful of basil
- One lemongrass stalk (sliced)
- Two red chilies
- Four garlic cloves
- One-inch piece of galangal (sliced)
- Three-fourth tsp. of each
- Coriander (ground)
- Turmeric
- Shrimp paste
- One and a half tbsp. of each
- Brown sugar
- Ketchup
- Two and a half tbsp. of each
- Lime juice

- Fish sauce
- One-eighth tsp. of cardamom (ground)

Method:

1. Place chilies, lemongrass, galangal, garlic, turmeric, shrimp paste, brown sugar, coriander, ketchup, lime juice, fish sauce, and cardamom in a blender. Add one-fourth can of the coconut milk. Blend well.

2. Heat the oil in a large wok. Add the onion rings. Fry for two minutes and add the stock. Simmer for two minutes. Reserve half of the onion rings in a bowl and leave the rest in the wok.

3. Add the beef. Fry for three minutes. Add the red wine.

4. Add the prepared paste along with the remaining coconut milk. Add the bay leaves. Add the chunks of pineapple and boil for two minutes.

5. Add the tomatoes along with the lime juice. Cook for two minutes.

6. Serve with Thai jasmine rice.

Slow-Cooker Thai Pork

Total Prep & Cooking Time: Eight hours and thirty minutes
Yields: Eight servings
Nutrition Facts: Calories: 210 | Protein: 18.9g | Carbs: 9.7g | Fat: 9.2g | Fiber: 2.6g

Ingredients

- Two red bell peppers (cut in strips)
- Four pork loin chops
- Half cup of teriyaki sauce
- One-fourth cup of each
  - Peanut butter (creamy)
  - Peanuts
- Two tbsps. of rice vinegar
- One tsp. of red pepper flakes
- Two garlic cloves (minced)
- One-third cup of green onions (chopped)
- Two limes (cut in wedges)

Method:

1. Use cooking spray for coating a slow cooker. Add the pork chops along with the strips of bell pepper to the cooker. Add the vinegar, teriyaki sauce, garlic, and pepper flakes over the chops.

2. Cook for eight hours on low. Add the peanut butter and stir well. Cook for ten minutes.

3. Serve with peanuts and green onions from the top.

**Thai Pork and Peanut Sauce**

Total Prep & Cooking Time: Twenty minutes
Yields: Four servings
Nutrition Facts: Calories: 361.3 | Protein: 18.9g |
Carbs: 15.6g | Fat: 24.9g | Fiber: 2.6g

Ingredients

- One-fourth cup of flour
- One tsp. of cumin (ground)
- One-fourth tsp. of cayenne pepper
- Half tsp. of salt
- Two tbsps. of vegetable oil
- Four pork chops
- One-third cup of chicken stock
- Half cup of coconut milk
- Two tbsps. of peanut butter
- One tbsp. of honey
- Two tsps. of ginger (ground)
- One-fourth cup of each
- Red bell pepper (sliced)
- Green onion (chopped)
- Peanuts
- Cilantro (chopped)

Method:

1. Combine cumin, flour, cayenne pepper, and half tsp. of salt on a flat dish. Mix well. Coat the pork with the mixture of flour.

2. Take a wok and heat the oil in it. Add the pork chops and cook for four minutes on each side.

3. Combine coconut milk, stock, honey, peanut butter, ginger, and salt.

4. Remove the pork chops from the wok and add the sauce. Cook for two minutes.

5. Serve the pork chops with peanut sauce from the top. Garnish with bell pepper, green onion, cilantro, and peanuts.

Thai Slow Cooker Pork and Pepper

Total Prep & Cooking Time: Five hours and thirty minutes
Yields: Four servings
Nutrition Facts: Calories: 312.3 | Protein: 21.2g | Carbs: 21.6g | Fat: 14.3g | Fiber: 2.9g

Ingredients

- One cup of chicken stock
- One-third cup of soy sauce
- Half cup of peanut butter (creamy)
- Three tbsps. of honey
- Six garlic cloves (minced)
- Two tbsps. of ginger (minced)
- One tsp. of red pepper flakes
- Two red bell peppers (sliced)
- One pound of pork chops (boneless)

Method:

1. Add soy sauce, chicken stock, honey, peanut butter, ginger, garlic, red bell peppers, pepper flakes, and pork chops in the slow cooker. Mix all the listed ingredients and cook on low.

2. Cook the pork for five hours. Remove the pork and shred it. Add it to the sauce. Cook for ten minutes.

3. Serve hot.

Ground Pork Skewers

Total Prep & Cooking Time: One hour and thirty-five minutes
Yields: Eight servings
Nutrition Facts: Calories: 260.3| Protein: 21.3g |
Carbs: 7.8g | Fat: 17.2g | Fiber: 0.2g

Ingredients

- Two pounds of pork (ground)
- One-fourth cup of white sugar
- Two tbsps. of fish sauce
- Six garlic cloves (minced)
- One tsp. of salt
- Half tsp. of black pepper (ground)
- Two tsps. of baking powder
- One tbsp. of water

Method:

1. Mix sugar, pork, fish sauce, salt, pepper, and garlic in a bowl. Combine the ingredients properly.

2. Combine the baking powder in one tbsp. of water. Add it to the mixture of pork. Let the marinated pork rest in the refrigerator for one hour.

3. Heat a grill pan and use some oil for greasing.

4. Take one handful of the mixture of pork and thread it to the skewer. Shape the skewer into sausage shape of one inch.

5. Add the skewers to the pan and grill for fifteen minutes on all sides.

6. Serve hot.

Pad Krapao (Stir-Fry Pork and Basil)

Total Prep & Cooking Time: Twenty-five minutes
Yields: Three servings
Nutrition Facts: Calories: 360.6 | Protein: 27.9g |
Carbs: 23.5g | Fat: 17.6g | Fiber: 3.3g

Ingredients

- Three tbsps. of vegetable oil
- Three garlic cloves (chopped)
- Three hot chili peppers (sliced)
- One and a half cup of pork (sliced)
- One tbsp. of each
- Sweet soy sauce
- Dark soy sauce
- Chili paste in soya bean oil
- Four tbsps. of fish sauce
- Two cups of white onion (sliced)
- Half cup of green bell pepper (sliced)
- One cup of basil leaves
- One tsp. of white pepper (ground)

Method:

1. Start by heating the oil in a large wok. Add the chili pepper and garlic to the wok. Cook for one minute. Add the sliced pork and cook for three minutes. Add the sweet soy sauce, dark soy sauce, and fish sauce. Cook for four minutes.

2. Add the onions, chili paste, and bell pepper. Stir-fry the mixture for six minutes. Add the basil leaves and add pepper for seasoning.

3. Serve hot.

Pork Red Curry With Squash

Total Prep & Cooking Time: Forty minutes
Yields: Two servings
Nutrition Facts: Calories: 710.3 | Protein: 25.6g |
Carbs: 37.9g | Fat: 51.6g | Fiber: 7.9g

Ingredients

- One tbsp. of each
- Vegetable oil
- Red curry paste
- Half pound of pork loin (sliced thinly)
- One can of coconut milk
- Three cups of butternut squash (cubed)
- Two cups of cabbage (chopped)
- Two tbsps. of fish sauce
- One and a half tbsp. of white sugar

Method:

1. Heat the oil in a pot. Add the curry paste. Fry for two minutes. Add the pork. Cook for five minutes.

2. Add the coconut milk. Boil the mixture.

3. Add the squash and reduce the flame. Simmer for ten minutes. Add the chopped cabbage and cook for five minutes.

4. Add sugar and fish sauce for seasoning.

5. Serve with jasmine rice.

KhanomJeeb (Shrimp and Pork Dumplings)

Total Prep & Cooking Time: One hour
Yields: Six servings
Nutrition Facts: Calories: 251.4 | Protein: 11.3g |
Carbs: 26.2g | Fat: 8.9g | Fiber: 1.9g

Ingredients

For the garlic oil:

- Three garlic cloves (minced)
- Three tbsps. of vegetable oil

For the wontons:

- Five black peppercorns
- Two garlic cloves
- One pinch of salt
- Two stems of cilantro (chopped)
- Five ounces of pork (ground)
- Four ounces of shrimp (minced)
- Five water chestnuts (minced)
- One tbsp. of each
- White sugar
- Dark soy sauce
- One tsp. of each
- Fish sauce
- White sugar
- Tapioca starch
- Light soy sauce

- Half tsp. of salt
- Twenty-five wonton wrappers

For the dipping sauce:

- Three tbsps. of each
- Light soy sauce
- Rice vinegar
- One tbsp. of white sugar
- Two scallions (sliced in rings)
- One chili pepper

Method:

1. Heat the oil in a large skillet. Add the garlic. Cook for five minutes. Remove the garlic from the skillet.

2. Crush the black peppercorns until powdery. Add the garlic and salt. Crush them for making a fine paste. Add the stems of cilantro and mix again.

3. Combine the paste, shrimp, pork, dark soy sauce, chestnuts, white sugar, tapioca starch, fish sauce, salt, and light soy sauce in a bowl. Take the wonton wrappers and spoon two tsps. of the pork mixture in the middle portion of each wrapper. Fold the wonton wrappers and seal the edges.

4. Steam the wontons for ten minutes.

5. Combine all the dipping sauce ingredients in a small bowl.

6. Serve the wontons with dipping sauce by the side and a drizzle of garlic oil from the top.

Thai Pork Coconut Curry

Total Prep & Cooking Time: Twenty-five minutes
Yields: Five servings
Nutrition Facts: Calories: 220.1 | Protein: 22.6g |
Carbs: 3.6g | Fat: 11.4g | Fiber: 0.6g

Ingredients

- One tbsp. of vegetable oil
- Three cups of coconut curry sauce
- Two pounds of lean pork (cut in cubes)

Method:

1. Take a large saucepan. Heat the oil in it. Add the pork cubes and cook for five minutes.

2. Add the coconut curry sauce and boil the mixture. Simmer for twenty minutes.

Thai Cashew Chicken

Total Prep & Cooking Time: Three hours
Yields: Four servings
Nutrition Facts: Calories: 680.3 | Protein: 32.6g |
Carbs: 67.2g | Fat: 27.3g | Fiber: 3.6g

Ingredients

- One-fourth cup of each
- Fish sauce
- Soy sauce
- Two tbsps. of hot pepper sauce
- Three garlic cloves (minced)
- One tbsp. of ginger (minced)
- Four chicken breasts (cut in strips)
- One cup of jasmine rice (dry)
- Three tbsps. of brown sugar
- One onion (sliced)
- Three-fourth cup of water
- Two and a half tbsp. of peanut butter (creamy)
- Half cup of cashew nuts

Method:

1. Mix fish sauce, soy sauce, hot pepper sauce, ginger, fish sauce, and garlic in a bowl. Add the chicken strips and marinate for two hours in the refrigerator.

2. Boil the jasmine rice with two cups of water in a saucepan. Simmer for twenty minutes.

3. Take a skillet and heat the oil in it. Add the brown sugar. Add the onion and cook for five minutes. Add the marinated chicken. Cook for ten minutes.

4. Add three-fourth cup of water to the skillet and boil.

5. Add the peanut butter and cook for ten minutes. Add the cashew nuts and stir.

6. Serve with jasmine rice by the side.

Thai Basil and Chicken Stir-Fry

Total Prep & Cooking Time: Thirty-five minutes
Yields: Six servings
Nutrition Facts: Calories: 493.1 | Protein: 34.6g |
Carbs: 58.3g | Fat: 13.6g | Fiber: 2.9g

Ingredients

- Two cups of jasmine rice (uncooked)
- Three-fourth cup of coconut milk
- Three tbsps. of each
- Rice wine vinegar
- Soy sauce
- Two tbsps. of fish sauce
- Three-fourth tsp. of pepper flakes
- One tbsp. of olive oil
- One onion (sliced)
- Two and a half tbsp. of ginger (minced)
- Three garlic cloves (minced)
- Two pounds of chicken breast (cut in strips)
- Three shitake mushrooms (sliced)
- Five green onions (chopped)
- One and a half cup of basil leaves

Method:

1. Boil the jasmine rice with water in a pot.
   Simmer for twenty minutes.

2. Mix soy sauce, coconut milk, fish sauce, rice
   wine vinegar, and pepper flakes in a bowl.

3. Take a wok and heat the oil. Add ginger, onion, and garlic. Cook for two minutes. Add the chicken in the wok. Cook for three minutes. Add the coconut milk. Keep cooking until the sauce thickens.

4. Add green onions, mushrooms, and basil. Cook for two minutes.

5. Serve with jasmine rice.

Chicken and Pineapple Curry

Total Prep & Cooking Time: Fifty minutes
Yields: Six servings
Nutrition Facts: Calories: 620.3 | Protein: 21.6g |
Carbs: 74.7g | Fat: 35.4g | Fiber: 4.5g

Ingredients

- One-fourth cup of red curry paste
- Two cans of coconut milk
- Two breasts of chicken (cut in strips)
- Three tbsps. of fish sauce
- One-fourth cup of white sugar
- One and a half cup of bamboo shoots (sliced)
- Half a red bell pepper (julienned)
- Half a green bell pepper (julienned)
- One onion (chopped)
- One cup of pineapple chunks

Method:

1. Whisk together the curry paste along with one can of coconut milk. Add this mixture to the wok.

2. Add the remaining coconut milk along with fish sauce, chicken, bamboo shoots, and sugar. Boil for fifteen minutes.

3. Add green bell pepper, onion, and red bell pepper in the wok. Cook for ten minutes.

4. Add the pineapples and let the chicken sit for two minutes.

5. Serve hot.

Thai Chicken Tenders

Total Prep & Cooking Time: Twelve minutes
Yields: Five servings
Nutrition Facts: Calories: 349.3 | Protein: 26.6g |
Carbs: 15.9g | Fat: 20.1g | Fiber: 3.7g

Ingredients

- Two tbsps. of sesame oil
- One pound of chicken (boneless, cut in strips)
- Two tsps. of ginger (minced)
- Half cup of hoisin sauce
- One cup of peanut butter (creamy)
- One tsp. of cayenne pepper
- One-third cup of scallions (chopped)

Method:

1. Heat the oil in a large skillet. Add the chicken. Cook for three minutes.

2. Add the hoisin sauce, ginger, peanut butter, and cayenne pepper. Cook for two minutes.

3. Sprinkle scallions from the top and stir.

4. Serve hot.

Thai-Style Barbeque Chicken

Total Prep & Cooking Time: Four hours and fifteen minutes
Yields: Six servings
Nutrition Facts: Calories: 311.2 | Protein: 30.7g | Carbs: 5.1g | Fat: 17.2g | Fiber: 0.8g

Ingredients

- One bunch of cilantro
- Three garlic cloves (peeled)
- Three red chili peppers (chopped)
- One tsp. of each
- Curry powder
- Turmeric (ground)
- One tbsp. of white sugar
- One pinch of salt
- Three tbsps. of fish sauce
- Three pounds of chicken (cut in small pieces)
- One-fourth cup of coconut milk

Method:

1. Combine the cilantro, chili peppers, garlic, curry powder, turmeric, salt, and sugar in a food processor. Add the fish sauce and keep blending until smooth.

2. Add the paste to the chicken and marinate for three hours.

3. Heat a grill pan. Grease it with some oil.

4. Add the chicken pieces to the grill. Brush them with coconut milk. Cook for fifteen minutes and turn in between. Cook until the chicken pieces are tender.

5. Serve immediately.

**Breaded Chicken Fillet**

Total Prep & Cooking Time: One hour
Yields: Ten servings
Nutrition Facts: Calories: 201.3 | Protein: 30.6g |
Carbs: 12.6g | Fat: 2.5g | Fiber: 2.6g

Ingredients

- Ten chicken breast halves
- Four green chili peppers (chopped)
- Five green onions (chopped)
- One tbsp. of lime zest
- Two limes (juiced)
- Three-fourth cup of cilantro
- Three tbsps. of fish sauce
- One lemongrass
- One tsp. of salt
- Two tsps. of white sugar
- One and a half tbsp. of each
- Parmesan cheese (grated)
- Dijon mustard
- Sesame seeds (toasted)
- One cup of bread crumbs
- Pepper and salt (for seasoning)

Method:

1. Combine green onions, peppers, lime juice, lime zest, half of the cilantro, lemongrass, fish sauce, sugar, salt, and mustard in a blender. Keep blending until smooth.

2. Cut the chicken into the desired size. Pour the marinade and combine it. Marinate for forty minutes.

3. Mix cilantro, breadcrumbs, cheese, salt, and sesame seeds in a bowl. Roll the chicken pieces in the mixture.

4. Add the chicken pieces in a greased baking tray. Bake them for twenty minutes at 175 degrees Celsius.

GkaiKamin

Total Prep & Cooking Time: Four hours and fifteen minutes
Yields: Four servings
Nutrition Facts: Calories: 402.3 | Protein: 37.9g | Carbs: 10.2g | Fat: 20.7g | Fiber: 2.8g

Ingredients

- One whole chicken
- Two stalks of lemongrass
- Twelve garlic cloves
- Two tbsps. of salt
- Five tbsps. of fresh turmeric (peeled, chopped)
- One tsp. of white peppercorns

Method:

1. Pound salt, lemongrass, turmeric, garlic, and pepper in a mortar and pestle. Make a very fine paste.

2. Cut the chicken lengthwise. Separate it into two pieces. Rub the chicken with the spice mix. Marinate for four hours in the refrigerator.

3. Grill the chicken for fifteen minutes.

4. Serve hot.

Thai-Style Sweet Chicken Bowl

Total Prep & Cooking Time: Fifty-five minutes
Yields: Six servings
Nutrition Facts: Calories: 624.5 | Protein: 20.6g |
Carbs: 89.6g | Fat: 23.6g | Fiber: 4.7g

Ingredients

- Three tbsps. of water
- One tsp. of salt
- Three chicken breast halves
- Half cup of soy sauce
- One can of coconut milk
- One cup of white sugar
- Two tbsps. of curry powder
- One mango (diced)
- Two and a half cup of clover sprouts
- One-third cup of cashews (chopped)
- One bunch of cilantro (chopped)
- Four green onions (chopped)

Method:

1. Add the chicken breasts in a pan along with soy sauce and one tbsp. of water. Cover and cook for twenty minutes. Cut the cooked chicken into cubes.

2. Mix sugar, coconut milk, and curry powder in a small saucepan. Simmer the mixture and add the mango cubes. Cook for five minutes.

3. Serve the chicken in serving plates and top with cilantro, cashews, sprouts, and green onions. Drizzle the mango sauce from the top.

Chicken Panang Curry

Total Prep & Cooking Time: Thirty-five minutes
Yields: Four servings
Nutrition Facts: Calories: 590.1 | Protein: 19.6g |
Carbs: 16.2g | Fat: 52.3g | Fiber: 3.6g

Ingredients

- One tbsp. of vegetable oil
- One-fourth cup of Panang curry paste
- Four cups of coconut milk
- Ten ounces of chicken breast (cubed)
- Two tbsps. of each
- Fish sauce
- Palm sugar
- Six leaves of kaffir lime (torn)
- Two red chili peppers (sliced)
- One bunch of basil leaves

Method:

1. Take a large wok and heat the oil in it. Add the curry paste and cook for five minutes. Add the coconut milk along with the chicken. Cook for five minutes. Add the palm sugar, lime leaves, and fish sauce. Simmer for five minutes.

2. Serve with basil and red chili peppers from the top.

Tamarind Chicken

Total Prep & Cooking Time: Twenty-five minutes
Yields: Two servings
Nutrition Facts: Calories: 445.2 | Protein: 42.3g |
Carbs: 24.6g | Fat: 16.2g | Fiber: 1.3g

Ingredients

- Three tbsps. of soy sauce
- Four tsps. of flour
- Fourteen ounces of chicken breast (cut in bite-size pieces)

For the tamarind sauce:

- One-third cup of water
- Two tbsps. of each
- Brown sugar
- Fish sauce
- Tamarind paste
- Olive oil
- Three garlic cloves (minced)
- One green chili pepper
- Half tsp. of ginger (grated)

Method:

1. Combine the flour and soy sauce in a bowl. Add the chicken and coat well.

2. Combine fish sauce, water, tamarind paste, and brown sugar in a bowl.

3. Heat the oil in a large wok. Add the chili pepper, garlic, and ginger. Cook for three minutes. Add the chicken and cook for two minutes.

4. Add half of the tamarind mixture and stir-fry for three minutes. Add the remaining sauce and cook for fifteen minutes.

5. Serve hot.

KhaiYat Sai (Thai Mushroom Stuffed Omelet)

Total Prep & Cooking Time: Thirty minutes
Yields: Two servings
Nutrition Facts: Calories: 223.6 | Protein: 16.5g |
Carbs: 12.3g | Fat: 10.7g | Fiber: 3.2g

Ingredients

- Half cup of mushrooms (sliced)
- Four scallions (chopped)
- One garlic clove (minced)
- Two sprigs of cilantro
- One Thai chili
- Two sprigs of Thai basil
- One tbsp. of tomato paste
- Four large eggs
- Two tbsps. of each
- Fish sauce
- Sesame seeds (black)
- Oyster sauce
- Vegetable oil
- Pepper and salt (for seasoning)

Method:

1. Take a frying pan and heat the oil. Add the mushrooms and sauté for two minutes. Add the remaining veggies and cook for two minutes. Add pepper and salt for seasoning along with the tomato paste.

2. Whisk the eggs along with sesame seeds, fish sauce, and chili.

3. Add the egg mixture to the pan and cook for two minutes on each side. Fold the omelet in half. Cook for two minutes.

4. Divide the omelet into two plates and serve hot with oyster sauce from the top.

Hoi Tod (Egg Pancakes With Mussels)

Total Prep & Cooking Time: Thirty minutes
Yields: Two servings
Nutrition Facts: Calories: 73.2 | Protein: 7.6g | Carbs:
5.3g | Fat: 4.6g | Fiber: 0.3g

Ingredients

- One cup of mussels (cooked)
- Half cup of bean sprouts
- Two tsps. of soy sauce
- One tsp. of fish sauce
- Two spring onions (chopped)
- One large egg
- Three tbsps. of cooking oil
- Two coriander stalks

For the pancake mixture:

- One-third cup of corn flour
- One and a half cup of flour
- Two cups of rice flour
- Five cups of water

Method:

1. Mix all the pancake mixture ingredients in a
   bowl. Make sure the consistency is loose and
   runny.

KhaiLukKhoei (Son-In-Law Egg)

Total Prep & Cooking Time: One hour
Yields: Four servings
Nutrition Facts: Calories: 570.2 | Protein: 7.6g |
Carbs: 24.6g | Fat: 47.6g | Fiber: 1.1g

Ingredients

- Eight boiled eggs (peeled)
- Half cup of shallots (fried)
- One cup of palm sugar (grated)
- One-fourth cup of fish sauce
- Two tbsps. of tamarind pulp
- Three tbsps. of water
- Two red chilies (sliced)
- Cilantro leaves (for garnishing)
- Vegetable oil (for frying)

Method:

1. Heat the oil in a large wok. Add the boiled eggs and fry them for five minutes. Remove the eggs and keep aside.

2. Take a pan and combine palm sugar, fish sauce, red chilies, tamarind pulp, and water. Simmer for three minutes.

3. Cut the fried eggs in half. Pour the prepared sauce over the halved eggs. Top with fried shallots.

4. Serve with cilantro from the top.

2. Heat a pan and add twp tbsps. of oil. Add some of the pancake mixture and swirl the pan for covering.

3. Arrange eight mussels on the pancake. Beat one egg along with some spring onions.

4. Add the egg mixture over the mussels. Cook for two minutes on each side. Flip carefully.

5. Sauté the bean sprouts in another pan for one minute. Add the fish sauce and soy sauce.

6. Serve the bean sprouts on the plates and top with the pancakes.

KhaiYat Say (Thai Stuffed Egg)

Total Prep & Cooking Time: Thirty minutes
Yields: Two servings
Nutrition Facts: Calories: 430.3 | Protein: 12.6g |
Carbs: 68.6g | Fat: 12.4g | Fiber: 3.9g

Ingredients

- Two large eggs
- Pepper and salt (for seasoning)
- Two tbsps. of each
- Carrot (diced)
- Green peas
- Onions (minced)
- One garlic clove (minced)
- One-hundred grams of pork (minced)
- One tbsp. of spring onions (minced)
- One tsp. of fish sauce

Method:

1. Heat oil in a wok. Add the carrots along with the onions.

2. Add the garlic. Cook for two minutes. Add the pork. Cook for five minutes.

3. Beat the eggs in a bowl. Add pepper and salt.

4. Remove the mince mixture from the wok and add the eggs.

5. Add the mince mixture to the center of the omelet. Fold the omelet from the sides.

6. Cook for two minutes.

Thai-Style Devilled Egg

Total Prep & Cooking Time: Thirty minutes
Yields: Sixteen servings
Nutrition Facts: Calories: 73.2 | Protein: 7.7g | Carbs: 5.1g | Fat: 6.8g | Fiber: 0.7g

Ingredients

- Eight large eggs (boiled, peeled)
- One tbsp. of sriracha sauce
- Two tbsps. of mayonnaise
- One and a half tbsp. of lime juice
- Two tsps. of fish sauce
- Red chili (sliced, for serving)
- Lime wedges (for serving)

Method:

1. Halve the eggs. Remove the egg yolks and keep in a bowl.

2. Add mayonnaise, sriracha sauce, fish sauce, and lime juice to the egg yolks. Use a spoon for mashing the yolks.

3. Spoon the mixture into the egg shells.

4. Serve with red chili and lime wedges from the top.

Pad Thai Egg Roll

Total Prep & Cooking Time: Forty-five minutes
Yields: Four servings
Nutrition Facts: Calories: 540.3 | Protein: 28.9g |
Carbs: 27.3g | Fat: 27.6g | Fiber: 9.1g

Ingredients

- Hundred grams of rice noodles
- Two tbsps. of lemon juice
- One tbsp. of fish sauce
- Half tbsp. of brown sugar
- Two and a half tbsp. of kecapmanis
- Three tbsps. of peanut oil
- Three-hundred grams of tofu (firm, cut in one-inch pieces)
- One carrot (ribboned)
- Half cup of green beans (chopped)
- Three green onions (sliced)
- Eight large eggs

Method:

1. Soak the noodles in hot water. Soak for ten minutes.

2. Mix fish sauce, sugar, lemon juice, and half of the kecapmanis in a bowl.

3. Take a wok and heat some oil in it. Add the tofu along with beans, carrots, and onions. Cook for

two minutes. Add the mixture of lemon juice. Add the noodles and stir.

4. Whisk the eggs in a bowl with two tbsps. of water.

5. Add two tsps. of oil in the wok. Add one tbsp. of the egg mixture and swirl for making a round. Repeat with the remaining batter.

6. Arrange the omelets on a plate. Add the noodle mixture in the center and roll the omelets.

7. Serve with coriander from the top.

Chapter 4: Vegetable Recipes

Apart from meat and non-vegetarian dish recipes, there are various Thai vegetable recipes that you can make at your home. This chapter is all about various types of vegetable recipes based on Thai cuisine.

Stir-Fried Bok Choy

Total Prep & Cooking Time: Fifteen minutes
Yields: Four servings
Nutrition Facts: Calories: 49 | Protein: 2.3g | Carbs: 3.6g | Fat: 3g | Fiber: 1.2g

Ingredients

- Five heads of bok choy (baby)
- One tbsp. of coconut oil

For the sauce:

- Four garlic cloves (minced)
- Two tbsps. of oyster sauce
- Three tbsps. of soy sauce
- One and a half tbsp. of fish sauce
- One tbsp. of sweet chili sauce
- Three-fourth tbsp. of brown sugar

Method:

1. Start by cutting the bottom portion of each bok choy head for separating the individual leaves.

2. Combine the sauce ingredients in a bowl. Mix well for dissolving the sugar.

3. Take a large wok and add oil in it. Add the bok choy along with three tbsps. of the sauce. Stir-fry the ingredients for two minutes. Continue adding a little bit of the sauce until the bok choy is cooked.

4. Serve the bok choy in serving plates with the wok juice all over the plate.

Stir-Fried Thai Veggies With Ginger, Garlic, and Lime

Total Prep & Cooking Time: Twenty minutes
Yields: Four servings
Nutrition Facts: Calories: 290 | Protein: 11.3g | Carbs: 41.3g | Fat: 11.9g | Fiber: 12.3g

Ingredients

- Two tbsps. of oil
- One-fourth cup of shallots (chopped)
- Six garlic cloves (minced)
- Two pieces of galangal (sliced in matchsticks)
- One red chili (sliced)
- One carrot (sliced)
- Six shitake mushrooms (sliced)
- One small head of cauliflower (cut in florets)
- One small broccoli (cut in florets)
- One red bell pepper (cut in strips)
- Three cups of bok choy (baby)
- Half cup of Thai basil

For the sauce:

- Two-third cup of coconut milk
- Three tbsps. of fish sauce
- One tbsp. of lime juice
- Half tsp. of chili flakes
- Two and a half tsp. of brown sugar

Method:

1. Mix fish sauce, coconut milk, chili flakes, lime juice, and brown sugar. Mix well for dissolving the sugar. Adjust the flavor by adding some lime juice and salt.

2. Take a wok and add two tbsps. of the oil. Add the garlic, chili, galangal, and shallots. Cook for two minutes.

3. Add mushrooms, carrots, cauliflower, broccoli, red pepper, and the sauce. Simmer the ingredients for two minutes. Add the bok choy. Simmer for two minutes by maintaining the crispness of the veggies.

4. Serve with basil leaves from the top.

Green Vegetable Curry

Total Prep & Cooking Time: Fifty minutes
Yields: Four servings
Nutrition Facts: Calories: 605.3 | Protein: 26.9g |
Carbs: 90.3g | Fat: 16.9g | Fiber: 21.4g

Ingredients

For the curry paste:

- One stalk of lemongrass (sliced)
- One tbsp. of coriander (ground)
- Two tsps. of cumin (ground)
- One and a half tbsp. of soy sauce
- Half tsp. of sugar
- Three green chilies (sliced)
- One-fourth cup of shallot
- Three garlic cloves two inches of galangal (grated)
- Two lime leaves (cut in thin strips)
- One cup of cilantro (chopped)
- One tsp. of salt

For the stir-fry:

- One can of coconut milk
- One cup of vegetable stock
- Two lime leaves
- Two cups of tofu (cut in cubes)
- One sweet potato (cubed)
- One zucchini (sliced)

- Half cup of snow peas
- Three tbsps. of oil

Method:

1. Add all the listed ingredients for the curry paste in a blender. Add one-third can of the coconut milk and blend until smooth.

2. Heat a pan. Drizzle some oil in it. Add the paste. Fry for two minutes.

3. Add the lime leaves along with the stock.

4. Simmer for two minutes. Add the tofu along with the sweet potato.

5. Simmer the mixture for ten minutes. Add the zucchini and bell pepper. Stir the ingredients and simmer for five minutes.

6. Lower the flame and add the remaining coconut milk. Cook for two minutes.

7. Serve in bowls with basil from the top.

Spaghetti Squash Pad Thai

Total Prep & Cooking Time: Forty-five minutes
Yields: Four servings
Nutrition Facts: Calories: 360 | Protein: 12.5g | Carbs: 31.3g | Fat: 23.9g | Fiber: 7.9g

Ingredients

- One spaghetti squash (cooked, filling scraped out)
- Half pound of tofu (cut in cubes of one-inch)
- Two tbsps. of fish sauce
- One and a half tbsp. of tamarind
- One tbsp. of sugar
- Half cup of cilantro
- Three tbsps. of oil
- Three scallions (sliced)
- One garlic clove (chopped)
- Two tbsps. of peanuts (chopped)
- Three ounces of bean sprouts
- One lime (cut in quarters)

Method:

1. Start by broiling the tofu cubes in a broiler by tossing with one tsp. of oil. Broil for eight minutes.

2. Take a bowl and mix tamarind, fish sauce, cilantro, sugar, and two tbsps. of water.

3. Heat a skillet and add the oil in it. Add the scallions along with the garlic. Sauté for one minute.

4. Add the bean sprouts. Cook for one minute. Add the sauce along with the spaghetti squash, tofu, and cilantro. Mix well for combining all the ingredients.

5. Serve with scallions from the top.

Thai Pumpkin Curry

Total Prep & Cooking Time: Thirty minutes
Yields: Four servings
Nutrition Facts: Calories: 480 | Protein: 15.6g | Carbs: 69.7g | Fat: 18.6g | Fiber: 15.4g

Ingredients

- One small pumpkin
- One small yam (cubed)
- Two carrots (cut in slices)
- One yellow bell pepper (cut in cubes)
- One cup of cherry tomatoes
- Half can of chickpeas
- Two tbsps. of orange zest

For the sauce:

- Four garlic cloves
- Two red chilies
- One can of coconut milk
- One tsp. of tamarind paste
- Two and a half tbsp. of soy sauce
- One tbsp. of each
- Lime juice
- Brown sugar
- Cumin
- Coriander (ground)
- Two tbsps. orange juice
- Half tsp. of turmeric
- One-third tbsp. of rice vinegar

- One onion (sliced)

Method:

1. Add all the sauce ingredients in a high power blender. Blend well.

2. Cut open the pumpkin and use a spoon for scooping out all the seeds. Cut the pumpkin in small cubes.

3. Add yam, carrots, and pumpkin in the wok. Add the curry sauce and stir-fry for two minutes.

4. Boil the mixture and simmer for six minutes.

5. Add cherry tomatoes, bell pepper, orange zest, and chickpeas. Simmer for three minutes.

6. Serve the curry with jasmine rice by the side.

Thai Coconut Curry

Total Prep & Cooking Time: Thirty minutes
Yields: Four servings
Nutrition Facts: Calories: 419 | Protein: 13.6g | Carbs: 40.3g | Fat: 23.9g | Fiber: 5.6g

Ingredients

For the curry:

- One tbsp. of coconut oil
- Two tbsps. of shallots (chopped)
- Half tbsp. of ginger (grated)
- Two and a half tbsp. of red curry paste
- Two cans of coconut milk
- One tsp. of vegetable bouillon
- Three tbsps. of each
- Honey
- Soy sauce
- One and a half tbsp. of chili garlic sauce

For the fillings:

- Four ounces of rice noodles
- One tbsp. of coconut oil
- Fourteen ounces of tofu (firm)
- One cup of each
- Red cabbage (sliced)
- Carrot (sliced)
- Snap peas

Method:

1. Heat oil in a wok. Add ginger and shallots. Cook for three minutes. Add the curry paste. Cook for two minutes. Add bouillon, coconut milk, honey, soy sauce, and chili garlic sauce. Simmer for five minutes.

2. Prepare the noodles by following the package instructions.

3. Cut the tofu in cubes and stir-fry them in a wok. Add a few tsps. of the curry and cook for two minutes. Keep aside.

4. Add cabbage, carrots, along with the snap peas to the wok. Cook for three minutes. Add the curry soup, noodles, and tofu. Combine well.

5. Serve immediately.

Battered Veggies With Thai Sauce

Total Prep & Cooking Time: Forty-five minutes
Yields: Eight servings
Nutrition Facts: Calories: 302.3 | Protein: 9.8g |
Carbs: 20.6g | Fat: 16.8g | Fiber: 1.3g

Ingredients

- Five cups of assorted vegetables of your choice (cut in bite-size pieces)
- Flour (for dusting)
- Vegetable oil (for frying)

For the batter:

- Two egg yolks
- Half cup of water
- Two-hundred grams of flour
- One tsp. of salt

For the Thai sauce:

- One tbsp. of each
- Coriander stems (chopped)
- Oil
- Fish sauce
- Two tsps. of garlic (minced)
- Three red chilies (chopped)
- One tsp. of ginger (chopped)
- Four tsps. of sugar
- Three tbsps. of soya sauce

- One lemon (juiced)

Method:

1. Mix flour, egg yolks, salt, and water. Mix well for making a smooth batter.

2. Use flour for dusting the veggies. Dip the vegetables in the batter.

3. Heat oil in a wok and deep fry the vegetables.

4. Heat some oil in another wok and add chilies, ginger, and fish sauce. Sauté the ingredients for two minutes. Add sugar, coriander, lemon juice, and soya sauce.

5. Serve the battered vegetables with Thai sauce by the side. You can also drizzle some sauce from the top.

Thai-Style Spicy Grilled Vegetable Skewers

Total Prep & Cooking Time: One hour and thirty minutes
Yields: Six servings
Nutrition Facts: Calories: 211.3 | Protein: 5.6g | Carbs: 21.2g | Fat: 13.6g | Fiber: 7.9g

Ingredients

- Two cups of cilantro leaves
- Eight garlic cloves (peeled)
- Two tbsps. of fish sauce
- One tbsp. of each
- Chili garlic sauce
- Water
- One tsp. of black pepper (ground)
- One-third cup of vegetable oil
- Two pounds of veggies (cut in bite-size pieces; any kind of combination of peppers, mushrooms, zucchini, summer squash, and scallion)

Method:

1. Add garlic, cilantro, water, fish sauce, pepper, and chili-garlic sauce in a blender. Pulse for making a fine paste.

2. Add the marinade to the veggies and combine them. Refrigerate for one hour.

3. Thread the veggies onto skewers.

4. Heat a grill pan. Grease the pan with some oil.

5. Grill the vegetable skewers for fifteen minutes.

6. Serve hot.

One-Pot Red Curry

Total Prep & Cooking Time: Thirty minutes
Yields: Four servings
Nutrition Facts: Calories: 329.3 | Protein: 5.7g |
Carbs: 24.7g | Fat: 25.3g | Fiber: 5.3g

Ingredients

- Two tbsps. of each
- Olive oil
- Tamari
- One onion (chopped)
- Half tsp. of salt
- Four garlic cloves (minced)
- Two and a half tbsp. of galangal (grated)
- Two carrots (chopped)
- Four ounces of red curry paste
- One cup of coconut milk
- Two cups of water
- One russet potato (diced in cubes of one-inch)
- One and a half cup of each
- Cauliflower florets
- Broccoli florets
- Half tbsp. of coconut sugar
- One-third tbsp. of lime juice

Method:

1. Heat oil in a large pot. Add garlic, onion, and ginger. Cook for two minutes. Add carrots and cook for five minutes.

2. Add coconut milk, curry paste, broccoli, potato, and cauliflower. Simmer the mixture for seven minutes.

3. Add coconut sugar, tamari, along with the lime juice.

4. Serve immediately with rice.

Thai Vegetable Chowder

Total Prep & Cooking Time: Thirty minutes
Yields: Four servings
Nutrition Facts: Calories: 89.4 | Protein: 7.2g | Carbs: 2.9g | Fat: 4.7g | Fiber: 5.1g

Ingredients

- Half tsp. of each
- Coriander seeds
- Red pepper flakes (crushed)
- One yellow onion (diced)
- Two cloves of garlic (minced)
- One tbsp. of ginger (minced)
- Two tbsps. of lemongrass (chopped)
- Three Thai chilies (minced)
- One cup of each
- Red bell pepper (diced)
- Carrots (diced)
- Milk
- Half cup of vegetable stock
- Four cups of corn kernels
- Two cups of each
- Oyster mushrooms
- Coconut water
- One tsp. tamari
- One-fourth cup of each
- Lime juice
- Cilantro leaves

Method:

1. Take a large pot and add coriander seeds, garlic, onion, lemongrass, ginger, and chilies. Cook for three minutes. Add bell pepper, carrots, and vegetable stock. Cook for five minutes.

2. Add corn kernels, red pepper flakes, milk, and coconut water. Boil the mixture and simmer for ten minutes.

3. Sauté mushrooms with tamari in a pan for two minutes.

4. Use a stick blender for blending the mixture. Blend until smooth.

5. Add the mushrooms and stir. Cook for two minutes.

6. Serve with lemon juice and cilantro from the top.

Pad Pak Boong (Stir-Fried Morning Glory)

Total Prep & Cooking Time: Fifteen minutes
Yields: Four servings
Nutrition Facts: Calories: 81 | Protein: 3.3 g | Carbs: 8.7g | Fat: 4.7g | Fiber: 1.8g

Ingredients

- One bunch of morning glory (cut in four-inch pieces)
- Four hot chilies
- Three garlic cloves (minced)
- Half tbsp. of each
- Yellow soya bean (paste)
- Soy sauce
- Oyster sauce
- One tbsp. of vegetable oil

Method:

1. Add the morning glory in a bowl along with the other ingredients. Do not put the oil.

2. Heat the oil in a wok and add the mixture of morning glory.

3. Toss the ingredients for two minutes.

4. Serve hot.

Pad Phuk Tong

Total Prep & Cooking Time: Fifteen minutes
Yields: Four servings
Nutrition Facts: Calories: 208 | Protein: 6.1g | Carbs: 16.7g | Fat: 18.9g | Fiber: 3.2g

Ingredients

- Two cups of pumpkin cubes (steamed)
- One tbsp. of garlic (chopped)
- Handful of basil
- Two tbsps. of cooking oil
- Half tsp. of each
- Fish sauce
- Pork broth powder
- Two tsps. of oyster sauce
- One tsp. of sugar
- Three tbsps. of water

Method:

1. Heat two tbsps. of oil in a large wok. Add garlic and cook for thirty seconds.

2. Add the pumpkin and toss.

3. Add the remaining ingredients. Mix well. Cook for two minutes.

4. Serve hot.

Eggplant Green Curry

Total Prep & Cooking Time: Thirty minutes
Yields: Four servings
Nutrition Facts: Calories: 382.1 | Protein: 12.6g |
Carbs: 46.3g | Fat: 17.2g | Fiber: 5.7g

Ingredients

- Two eggplants (cut in bite-size pieces)
- Half cup of vegetable oil
- One red bell pepper (sliced in sticks)
- One can bamboo shoots
- Half cup of coconut milk
- One stalk of lemongrass (cut in three pieces)
- Three lime leaves
- One tbsp. of fish sauce
- Half tbsp. of brown sugar
- One-fourth cup of basil
- Three chilies
- Green curry paste

Method:

1. Add oil in a wok and heat it. Add eggplants and cook for four minutes.

2. Heat another wok and add oil in it. Add curry paste along with coconut milk. Simmer for thirty minutes.

3. Add lime leaves, lemongrass, brown sugar, and fish sauce. Boil the mixture.

4. Add the bamboo shoots, bell pepper, and cooked eggplant. Cook for five minutes.

5. Serve with basil from the top.

Are you enjoying this book? If so, I' d really happy if you could leave a short review, it means lot to me! Thank you.

Chapter 5: Seafood Recipes

Seafood is an integral part of Thai cuisine. There are various simple yet tasty Thai recipes that can be made with seafood. Let's have a look at them.

Thai Fish Cakes

Total Prep & Cooking Time: One hour
Yields: Eight servings
Nutrition Facts: Calories: 164.1 | Protein: 12.6g |
Carbs: 10.9g | Fat: 6.8g | Fiber: 1.7g

Ingredients

- One pound of whitefish
- Half cup of flour
- Two tbsps. of each
- Sweet chili sauce
- Oyster sauce
- One tsp.of each
- Brown sugar
- Fish sauce
- One-fourth cup of cilantro
- Four spring onions
- One egg
- One cup of oil (for frying)

Method:

1. Mix half a cup of flour, fish, fish sauce, sweet chili sauce, oyster sauce, cilantro, spring onion,

along with egg in a blender. Keep blending until the ingredients are combined properly. Keep in the refrigerator for thirty minutes.

2. Shape the mixture of fish into patties. Dust them with some flour.

3. Heat the oil in a heavy skillet. Start frying the fish cakes. Fry for eight minutes and flip them once in the middle.

4. Serve hot.

Spicy Pepper and Garlic Shrimp

Total Prep & Cooking Time: Thirty-five minutes
Yields: Two servings
Nutrition Facts: Calories: 390.3 | Protein: 12.1g |
Carbs: 11.5g | Fat: 33.6g | Fiber: 3.6g

Ingredients

- Three tbsps. of oil
- One-fourth cup of water
- One cup of cabbage
- One tbsp. of garlic (minced)
- Eight shrimps
- Two tsps. of each
- Onion (minced)
- Red pepper
- One and a half tbsp. of cilantro
- One-third tbsp. of soy sauce

Method:

1. Take a heavy skillet and heat one tbsp. of oil in it.

2. Chop the cabbage and add it to the skillet. Add one tbsp. of water. Stir-fry the cabbage for thirty seconds. Keep aside.

3. Heat the leftover oil in the skillet. Add the shrimp along with the garlic. Stir-fry for two minutes. Add onion, red pepper, soy sauce,

cilantro, and the leftover water. Cook for
twenty seconds.

4. Arrange the cooked cabbage on a serving plate.

5. Top with the cooked shrimp. Serve hot.

Thai-Style Crab Rice

Total Prep & Cooking Time: Fifty-five minutes
Yields: Four servings
Nutrition Facts: Calories: 301.3 | Protein: 9.3g |
Carbs: 35.2g | Fat: 10.7g | Fiber: 2.9g

Ingredients

- Half cup of rice
- Two cups of water
- Three tbsps. of oil
- Two onions (chopped)
- Three garlic cloves (minced)
- Half tbsp. of sugar
- Two tsps. of salt
- One large egg
- One-fourth pound of crab (cooked)
- Three scallions (chopped)
- One tbsp. of cilantro
- One medium-sized cucumber (sliced)
- One lime

Method:

1. Start by boiling the rice in the water in a large pot. Simmer for twenty minutes.

2. Heat oil in a steel wok. Add the garlic along with the spring onions. Stir-fry for two minutes.

3. Add sugar, rice, and salt. Cook for five minutes. Mix well. Crack the egg in the middles for combining with the rice.

4. Add the crabmeat, scallions, and cilantro. Toss for combining. Cook for five minutes.

5. Garnish the fried rice with slices of lime and cucumber.

Thai-Style Shrimp Burger

Total Prep & Cooking Time: Thirty-five minutes
Yields: Four servings
Nutrition Facts: Calories: 468.8 | Protein: 41.3g |
Carbs: 30.1g | Fat: 18.6g | Fiber: 3.9g

Ingredients

- Two pounds of shrimp
- Two garlic cloves
- Two tbsps. of ginger root (chopped)
- One jalapeno pepper
- Six tbsps. of cilantro
- Three spring onions
- Half cup of peanut sauce
- One-fourth cup of bread crumbs
- Half tsp. of salt
- Two tbsps. of each
- Oil
- Lime juice
- Two cups of coleslaw mix
- Four pita bread

Method:

1. Add the shrimp in a food processor and pulse.
   Pulse until the shrimps are chopped properly.
   Transfer the chopped shrimp to a bowl.

2. Add ginger, garlic, spring onions, cilantro, one-
   fourth cup of peanut butter, salt, and bread
   crumbs. Combine the ingredients using a fork.

3. Divide the mixture into four portions. Use your hand for flattening the shrimp patties.

4. Take a bowl and whisk together lime juice, peanut butter, and oil. Toss the coleslaw with the prepared dressing.

5. Take a grill pan. Brush it with some oil. Add the shrimp patties and cook for four minutes on each side.

6. Grill the pita bread. Split them crosswise.

7. Add the patties on the bread halves. Top with coleslaw. Add the other halves of the bread and serve.

Thai Basil Rolls With Peanut and Hoisin Sauce

Total Prep & Cooking Time: Fifty minutes
Yields: Twelve servings
Nutrition Facts: Calories: 193.2 | Protein: 9.1g | Carbs: 27.2g | Fat: 4.1g | Fiber: 1.9g

Ingredients

For the rolls:

- Half pound of shrimp
- One pound of pork
- Eight ounces of rice noodles
- Twelve rice wrappers
- One bunch of basil
- One cup of cilantro
- Half cup of mint leaves
- Two cups of bean sprouts

For the sauce:

- One cup of hoisin sauce
- One tbsp. of peanut butter
- One and a half tbsp. of water
- One-fourth cup of peanuts (roasted. chopped)

Method:

1. Boil water in a large pot with a little bit of salt. Add the shrimps and cook for three minutes.

Drain the water and dry the shrimps. Slice the shrimps in half.

2. Boil some water again in a pot with a little bit of salt. Add the pork and boil for ten minutes. Drain the water and slice the pork into very thin strips.

3. Cook the noodles in boiling water for eight minutes. Drain the water and keep aside.

4. Fill a bowl with some warm water. Dip the wrappers in the warm water. Soak for thirty seconds.

5. Arrange the wrappers flat on a working surface. Add two basil leaves in the center. Add four shrimp halves on the basil leaves along with a small amount of pork.

6. Add some noodles and sprinkle mint, cilantro, and bean sprouts. Roll the wrappers from one side and tuck in the openings for making a tight roll. Repeat with the remaining wrappers.

7. Mix peanut butter, water, and hoisin sauce in a saucepan. Boil for two minutes and keep aside.

8. Serve the wrappers with dipping sauce by the side and garnish with chopped peanuts.

Steamed Mussels

Total Prep & Cooking Time: Thirty minutes
Yields: Six servings
Nutrition Facts: Calories: 480.1 | Protein: 46.9g |
Carbs: 20.4g | Fat: 23.4g | Fiber: 1.9g

Ingredients

- Five pounds of mussels
- One-third cup of lime juice
- One can of coconut milk
- Half cup of white wine
- One and a half tbsp. of red curry paste
- Two tbsps. of garlic (minced)
- One tbsp. of fish sauce
- Half tbsp. of sugar
- Two cups of cilantro (chopped)

Method:

1. Combine coconut milk, lime juice, curry paste, white wine, fish sauce, sugar, and garlic in a pot. Boil over a high flame and stir for dissolving the sugar. Boil the mixture for two minutes.

2. Add the mussels and cook for eight minutes until the mussels open.

3. Remove the pot from the heat and remove any unopened mussels.

4. Serve the mussels along with the liquid in serving dish. Garnish with cilantro.

Thai Tilapia

Total Prep & Cooking Time: Thirty-five minutes
Yields: Four servings
Nutrition Facts: Calories: 180.4 | Protein: 23.2g |
Carbs: 2.9g | Fat: 7.6g | Fiber: 0.9g

Ingredients

- Half cup of coconut milk
- Six almonds
- Two tbsps. of onion (minced)
- One tsp. of ginger (grated)
- Half tsp. of turmeric (ground)
- One and a half tsp. of lemongrass
- One-fourth tsp. of salt
- Four tilapia fillets
- One pinch of salt
- Half tsp. of red pepper flakes

Method:

1. Add almonds, coconut milk, onion, turmeric, ginger, salt, and lemongrass in a food processor. Blend until smooth.

2. Heat some oil in an iron skillet.

3. Season the fillets of tilapia with pepper and salt on all sides. Add the fillets in the skillet with the skin-side up.

4. Add the prepared sauce over the fillets of fish. Coat the fish fillets evenly with the help of a spatula. Add red pepper flakes.

5. Simmer the fish for fifteen minutes by covering the skillet.

6. Serve hot.

Thai Shrimp

Total Prep & Cooking Time: Thirty minutes
Yields: Four servings
Nutrition Facts: Calories: 287.3 | Protein: 19.5g |
Carbs: 8.1g | Fat: 19.4g | Fiber: 2.6g

Ingredients

- Four garlic cloves
- One-inch of galangal root
- One jalapeno pepper
- Half tsp. of salt
- One tsp. of turmeric
- Two tbsps. of oil
- One onion (chopped)
- One pound of shrimp
- Two tomatoes (chopped)
- One cup of coconut milk
- Three tbsps. of basil leaves (chopped)

Method:

1. Mix galangal, garlic, turmeric, jalapeno, and salt in a blender. Process the ingredients for making a fine paste. Keep aside.

2. Heat the oil in a large skillet. Add the onions. Cook for two minutes. Add the prepared spice paste. Cook for two minutes.

3. Add the shrimp. Cook for three minutes. Add the coconut milk along with the tomatoes.

Cover the skillet and simmer the mixture for five minutes.

4. Remove the lid. Cook for five more minutes.

5. Add the chopped basil.

6. Serve hot.

Shrimp Pad Thai

Total Prep & Cooking Time: One hour
Yields: Four servings
Nutrition Facts: Calories: 539.4 | Protein: 21.3g |
Carbs: 67.8g | Fat: 21.2g | Fiber: 6.7g

Ingredients

- Eight ounces of rice noodles
- Two tsps. of oil
- One onion (chopped)
- One tsp. of garlic (minced)
- Twelve shrimps
- One tbsp. of each
- Ketchup
- Fish sauce
- Sugar
- Lemon juice
- White wine vinegar
- Two large eggs
- One-fourth pounds of bean sprouts
- Half cup of peanuts (roasted)
- One lemon
- One-third cup of cilantro

Method:

1. Soak the noodles for fifteen minutes in cold
   water. Drain the noodles and cover them with
   hot water for fifteen minutes. Drain the water
   and keep aside.

2. Take a steel wok and heat some oil in it. Add the garlic and onion. Cook for five minutes. Add the shrimp. Cook for five minutes. Add fish sauce, ketchup, lemon juice, sugar, and vinegar. Add the eggs. Cook for two minutes.

3. Add the soaked noodles and toss. Add peanuts and bean sprouts.

4. Serve hot.

Shrimp Red Curry

Total Prep & Cooking Time: Forty Minutes
Yields: Four servings
Nutrition Facts: Calories: 429.9 | Protein: 14.5g |
Carbs: 7.8g | Fat: 44.8g | Fiber: 2.8g

Ingredients

- Two cans of coconut milk
- Two tbsps. of red curry paste
- One tbsp. of fish sauce
- One hot chili pepper (minced)
- Twenty-four shrimps

Method:

1. Take a large wok and mix curry paste, coconut milk, minced pepper, and fish sauce. Simmer the mixture on low flame for ten minutes.

2. Add the shrimps and cook for fifteen minutes.

3. Serve hot with rice.

Thai Monkfish Curry

Total Prep & Cooking Time: One hour
Yields: Three servings
Nutrition Facts: Calories: 410.3 | Protein: 21.3g |
Carbs: 10.6g | Fat: 35.1g | Fiber: 3.7g

Ingredients

- One tbsp. of peanut oil
- Half onion (chopped)
- One red bell pepper (chopped)
- Three tbsps. of curry paste
- One can of coconut milk
- Twelve ounces of monkfish
- One tbsp. of fish sauce
- Two tbsps. of each
- Lime juice
- Cilantro (chopped)

Method:

1. Heat the peanut oil in a large pan. Add the onions and cook for five minutes.

2. Add the red bell pepper. Cook for five minutes.

3. Add the curry paste and mix well. Add the coconut milk and stir.

4. Simmer the mixture for two minutes.

5. Add the cubes of monkfish and simmer the curry for ten minutes. Add the lime juice and fish sauce. Cook for two minutes.

6. Serve hot with rice.

Grilled Prawns and Spicy Lime-Peanut Vinaigrette

Total Prep & Cooking Time: One hour and twenty minutes
Yields: Eight servings
Nutrition Facts: Calories: 530.9 | Protein: 28.9g | Carbs: 14.6g | Fat: 30.7g | Fiber: 2.2g

Ingredients

- One-fourth cup of each
- Lemongrass
- Galangal root (minced)
- Lime juice
- Mirin sauce
- Vinegar
- Two tbsps. of garlic (minced)
- One-fourth tbsp. of cilantro
- One green chili (minced)
- Three-fourth cup of peanut oil
- Two pounds of shrimp
- Three tbsps. of lime zest
- Two tsps. of fish sauce
- Two Thai green chilies (minced)
- Two and a half tsp. of garlic (minced)
- Half cup of peanut butter
- One-third cup of peanut oil
- One tbsp. of cilantro (chopped)
- Three-fourth cup of peanuts (roasted)
- One pinch of salt

Method:

1. Combine half of the ginger, lemongrass, cilantro, garlic, oil, and one minced chili. Add the shrimps and toss for coating. Marinate the shrimps for thirty minutes.

2. Heat a grill pan.

3. Add lime juice, mirin, vinegar, soy sauce, and water in a food processor. Add one tbsp. of ginger, two chili peppers, fish sauce, lime zest, peanut butter, and garlic. Blend the ingredients until smooth. Slowly add peanut oil while blending. Add cilantro and chopped peanuts. Keep aside.

4. Grill the marinated shrimps for two minutes on each side.

5. Serve the grilled shrimps with vinaigrette by the side.

Steamed Crab Leg With Lemongrass

Total Prep & Cooking Time: Thirty minutes
Yields: Two servings
Nutrition Facts: Calories: 580.6 | Protein: 87.3g |
Carbs: 5.1g | Fat: 19.2g | Fiber: 0.6g

Ingredients

- Two tbsps. of oil
- Three garlic cloves (minced)
- One-inch of galangal
- One stalk of lemongrass
- Two and a half tbsp. of fish sauce
- One tbsp. of oyster sauce
- One pinch of salt
- Two pounds of crab legs (cooked)

Method:

1. Take a large pot and heat it over medium heat. Add the oil.

2. Add ginger, garlic, and lemongrass to the oil. Cook for two minutes. Add the oyster sauce, fish sauce, pepper, and salt.

3. Add the legs of crab and cook for fifteen minutes. Stir well.

4. Serve hot.

Grilled Mahi Mahi With Thai Coconut Sauce

Total Prep & Cooking Time: Thirty minutes
Yields: Two servings
Nutrition Facts: Calories: 490.2 | Protein: 31.6g |
Carbs: 8.6g | Fat: 32.6g | Fiber: 2.8g

Ingredients

- Two cups of coconut milk
- Two tbsps. of cilantro (chopped)
- Three tbsps. of scallions (chopped)
- Two and a half tbsp. of lime juice
- Four tsps. of ginger (grated)
- Two garlic cloves (minced)
- One tsp. of fish sauce
- Two fillets of mahi-mahi

Method:

1. Heat the grill pan.

2. Add cilantro, coconut milk, scallions, garlic, lime juice, ginger, and fish sauce in a medium-sized saucepan. Boil the mixture.

3. Brush the fillets of mahi-mahi with the prepared sauce. Boil the remaining sauce until thickened.

4. Add the fillets of mahi-mahi to the grill pan. Cook for seven minutes on each side.

5. Serve the grilled fish fillets with sauce from the top.

Thai-Style Green Curry Prawns

Total Prep & Cooking Time: Forty minutes
Yields: Four servings
Nutrition Facts: Calories: 530.2 | Protein: 21.7g |
Carbs: 16.6g | Fat: 40.3g | Fiber: 7.9g

Ingredients

- Half tsp. of cumin
- One and a half tsp. of coriander seeds
- One tbsp. of ginger (grated)
- Four tsps. of garlic (minced)
- Two green chili peppers
- Three stalks of lemongrass
- One-third cup of cilantro
- Two tbsps. of lime juice
- One tbsp. of lime zest
- Three tbsps. of oil
- Half pound of beans
- One can of baby corn
- One-fourth tbsp. of soy sauce
- One can of coconut milk
- Three-fourth pounds of shrimp

Method:

1. Add ginger, coriander, cumin, green chili peppers, garlic, cilantro, lemongrass, lime zest, lime juice, and two tbsps. of oil in a high power blender. Blend for making a smooth paste.

2. Add the remaining oil in an iron skillet. Add the beans along with the baby corns. Cook for thirty seconds.

3. Add the prepared paste, coconut milk, and soy sauce. Boil the mixture.

4. Simmer for seven minutes and add the shrimps.

5. Cook for five minutes.

6. Serve hot with rice.

Thai Fried Prawns With White Pepper and Garlic

Total Prep & Cooking Time: Ten minutes
Yields: Four servings
Nutrition Facts: Calories: 370.2 | Protein: 20.6g |
Carbs: 17.6g | Fat: 26.9g | Fiber: 1.6g

Ingredients

- Eight garlic cloves (minced)
- Two tbsps. of flour
- Three tbsps. of fish sauce
- Two and a half tbsp. of soy sauce
- One tbsp. of sugar
- Half tsp. of white pepper
- One-fourth cup of oil
- One pound of shrimp

Method:

1. Mix garlic, flour, soy sauce, fish sauce, white pepper, and sugar in a large bowl. Add the prawns for coating.

2. Heat the oil in a pan. Add the prawns. Cook for two minutes.

3. Serve hot.

Thai Clam and Shrimp Curry

Total Prep & Cooking Time: Forty-five minutes
Yields: Four servings
Nutrition Facts: Calories: 320.6 | Protein: 11.6g |
Carbs: 12.5g | Fat: 27.3g | Fiber: 3.2g

Ingredients

- Two tbsps. of oil
- One onion (chopped)
- One red bell pepper
- One tbsp. of ginger (minced)
- Two garlic cloves (minced)
- One tsp. of chili paste
- One can of coconut milk
- Four large clams
- One-fourth cup of chicken stock
- One tsp. of each
- Brown sugar
- Fish sauce
- Three tbsps. of basil
- Twelve shrimps
- One lime

Method:

1. Heat oil in a large pan. Add red bell pepper and onion. Cook for four minutes. Add garlic and ginger. Cook for two minutes.

2. Add the chili paste along with coconut milk. Stir well.

3. Add the clams. Cook for five minutes. Grate some zest from the lime and mix. Add some lemon juice.

4. Add the shrimp and basil. Cook for ten minutes. Add chicken stock for adjusting the consistency.

5. Remove the clams.

6. Serve the curry with basil and lime zest.

Whole Fried Tilapia With Chilies and Basil

Total Prep & Cooking Time: Thirty-five minutes
Yields: Four servings
Nutrition Facts: Calories: 330.3 | Protein: 14.6g |
Carbs: 9.6g | Fat: 31.3g | Fiber: 1.6g

Ingredients

- One whole tilapia fish
- Oil for frying
- Five red chili peppers
- Six garlic cloves (minced)
- One onion (chopped)
- Two tbsps. of each
- Soy sauce
- Fish sauce
- One-fourth cup of each
- Cilantro (chopped)
- Basil (chopped)

Method:

1. Heat the oil in a large pan.

2. Clean the fish and make various slits on it using a sharp knife.

3. Add the fish to the oil. Fry for ten minutes. Remove from the oil. Drain excess oil.

4. Heat some oil in a skillet and add garlic, onion, and chili peppers. Cook for seven minutes.

5. Add soy sauce and fish sauce. Add cilantro and basil. Mix well.

6. Serve the fish on a plate and pour the prepared sauce all over the fish.

Chapter 6: Soupand Salad Recipes

Thai soups and salads are loaded with a punch of flavor that can make your dining experience even more interesting. The ingredients used are very simple. However, the flavors are extraordinary. In this chapter, you will find various Thai soup and salad recipes that can be made in no time.

Tom Yum Koong Soup

Total Prep & Cooking Time: One hour and ten minutes
Yields: Five servings
Nutrition Facts: Calories: 94.3 | Protein: 12.6g | Carbs: 11.3g | Fat: 1.4g | Fiber: 2.6g

Ingredients

- Half pound of shrimps
- Twelve mushrooms
- One can of canned mushrooms
- Four cups of water
- Two lemongrass
- Four leaves of kaffir lime
- Four slices of galangal
- Four bird's eye chili
- Two tbsps. of soy sauce
- One lime
- One tsp. of each
- Sugar
- Chili paste

- One tbsp. of tom yum soup paste

Method:

1. Start by trimming the lemongrass. Cut them into matchstick pieces.

2. For making the stock, add the shells and heads of the shrimps to water. Cook them for twenty minutes. Turn off the heat. Let the shells and heads soak for twenty minutes. Discard the heads and shells.

3. Add lemongrass, stock, galangal, kaffir lime leaves, chili paste, lime juice, fish sauce, chili, and sugar in a pot. Boil the mixture. After boiling the mixture for five minutes, add the mushrooms and shrimps.

4. Cook the soup for ten minutes.

5. Serve the soup hot and garnish with leaves of coriander.

Thai-Style Hot and Sour Soup

Total Prep & Cooking Time: Twenty-five minutes
Yields: Six servings
Nutrition Facts: Calories: 71.6 | Protein: 9.3g | Carbs: 4.6g | Fat: 1.7g | Fiber: 0.9g

Ingredients

- Three cups of chicken stock
- One tbsp. of tom yum soup paste
- Half garlic clove (minced)
- Three stalks of lemongrass
- Two leaves of kaffir lime
- Two breasts of chicken
- Four ounces of mushrooms
- One and a half tbsp. of fish sauce
- Two tbsps. of lime juice
- One tsp. of green chili pepper
- One bunch of coriander
- One sprig of basil

Method:

1. Boil the chicken stock in a large-sized saucepan. Add the soup paste along with the garlic. Cook the mixture for two minutes. Add the lime leaves and lemongrass.

2. Add the chicken breasts to the saucepan. Cook for five minutes on each side. Use a fork for shredding the chicken.

3. Add the mushrooms along with lime juice, fish sauce, and chili pepper.

4. Cook for eight minutes.

5. Serve the soup hot with basil and coriander garnish.

Thai Coconut Soup

Total Prep & Cooking Time: One hour and five minutes
Yields: Eight servings
Nutrition Facts: Calories: 360.3 | Protein: 13.1g | Carbs: 8.7g | Fat: 30.9g | Fiber: 2.3g

Ingredients

- One tbsp. of oil
- Two tbsps. of galangal root (minced)
- One stalk of lemongrass
- Two tsps. of curry paste
- Four cups of chicken stock
- Three tbsps. of fish sauce
- One and a half tbsp. of brown sugar
- Three cans of coconut milk
- Half pound of shiitake mushrooms
- One pound shrimp
- Two and a half tbsp. of lime juice
- One pinch of salt
- Half cup of cilantro

Method:

1. Heat oil in a pot. Add the lemongrass, galangal, and curry paste.

2. Add the chicken stock and mix well. Add the brown sugar along with the fish sauce. Simmer the mixture for fifteen minutes.

3. Add the mushrooms along with the coconut milk. Cook for five minutes until the mushrooms are tender.

4. Add the shrimps and cook for five minutes.

5. Taste and season using salt. Stir in the lime juice.

6. Garnish the soup with cilantro. Serve hot.

Tangy Prawn Soup

Total Prep & Cooking Time: Thirty-five minutes
Yields: Four servings
Nutrition Facts: Calories: 180.3 | Protein: 25.6g |
Carbs: 14.2g | Fat: 2.4g | Fiber: 2.6g

Ingredients

- One pound of tiger prawns
- Four cups of chicken stock
- Three stalks of lemongrass
- Three tbsps. of fish sauce
- One-fourth cup of lime juice
- Two tbsps. of spring onions (chopped)
- Ten leaves of kaffir lime
- One cup of canned mushrooms (rinsed)
- One tbsp. of cilantro
- Four red chili peppers (chopped)

Method:

1. Remove the prawn shells and devein them.

2. Rinse the prawn shells and add them to a saucepan. Add chicken stock.

3. Bruise the stalks of lemongrass and add them to the pan. Add half of the kaffir lime leaves. Boil the mixture and simmer for five minutes.

4. Strain the prepared stock and remove the solids.

5. Boil the stock again with prawns and mushrooms.

6. Add the lime juice, fish sauce, spring onions, red chilies, cilantro, and lime leaves.

7. Taste the soup and adjust the seasonings. The soup needs to be spicy, salty, sour, and hot.

8. Serve the soup with spring onion garnishing.

Spicy Vegetable Soup

Total Prep & Cooking Time: One hour and thirty minutes
Yields: Twelve servings
Nutrition Facts: Calories: 180.3 | Protein: 4.3g | Carbs: 20.3g | Fat: 6.5g | Fiber: 3.1g

Ingredients

- One cup of brown rice
- Two cups of water
- Three tbsps. of olive oil
- One onion
- Four garlic cloves (minced)
- One-fourth cup of ginger root (grated)
- One cup of carrot (cubed)
- Four cups of broccoli (florets)
- One red bell pepper (cubed)
- One can of coconut milk
- Six cups of vegetable stock
- One and a half cup of white wine
- Two tbsps. of soy sauce
- Three green chilies (chopped)
- Two and a half tbsp. of lemongrass (chopped)
- One-third tbsp. of pepper garlic sauce
- One tsp. of saffron
- Three-fourth cup of yogurt
- One bunch of cilantro (chopped)

Method:

1. Boil the brown rice with some water in a large pot. Simmer for forty minutes.

2. Heat olive oil in a pot. Add garlic, onion, ginger, and carrots. Cook for five minutes.

3. Add red bell pepper, broccoli, stock, coconut milk, fish sauce, white wine, chili peppers, soy sauce, garlic sauce, lemongrass, and saffron. Mix well. Simmer the mixture for twenty-five minutes.

4. Add the soup into a food processor in batches and blend until creamy and smooth.

5. Return the blended soup to the pot. Add the cooked rice. Add yogurt and mix well.

6. Garnish with cilantro. Serve hot.

Tom Ka Gai (Coconut Chicken Soup)

Total Prep & Cooking Time: One hour
Yields: Four servings
Nutrition Facts: Calories: 248.6 | Protein: 15.3g |
Carbs: 9.1g | Fat: 14.6g | Fiber: 2.8g

Ingredients

- Two tsps. of oil
- Two garlic cloves (minced)
- Two tbsps. of ginger root (grated)
- One-fourth cup of lemongrass (chopped)
- Two and a half tsp. of red pepper flakes (dried)
- One tsp. of each
- Cumin (ground)
- Coriander seed (ground)
- One breast of chicken (cut in strips)
- One onion (chopped)
- Two cups of bok choy
- Four cups of water
- One can of coconut milk
- One-third cup of fish sauce
- Three-fourth cup of cilantro (chopped)

Method:

1. Heat oil in a large-sized saucepan. Add ginger, garlic, red pepper flakes, lemongrass, cumin, and coriander. Cook for two minutes until fragrant.

2. Add the chicken pieces along with the onion. Cook for five minutes.

3. Add the bok choy and cook for ten minutes.

4. Add coconut milk, water, cilantro, and fish sauce. Simmer for thirty minutes.

5. Serve hot.

Thai Ginger Soup

Total Prep & Cooking Time: Twenty-five
Yields: Four servings
Nutrition Facts: Calories: 413.2 | Protein: 13.4g |
Carbs: 7.1g | Fat: 37.8g | Fiber: 2.9g

Ingredients

- Three cups of coconut milk
- Two cups of water
- Half pound of chicken breast (cut in strips)
- Three tbsps. of galangal root (minced)
- Two tbsps. of fish sauce
- One-fourth cup of lime juice
- Two and a half tbsp. of scallions (chopped)
- One tbsp. of cilantro (chopped)

Method:

1. Add water and coconut milk in a large
   saucepan. Boil the mixture.

2. Add the strips of chicken and simmer for three
   minutes.

3. Add fish sauce, galangal, and lime juice. Add
   the cilantro and scallions.

4. Serve hot.

Thai-Style Pumpkin Soup

Total Prep & Cooking Time: Twenty-five minutes
Yields: Four servings
Nutrition Facts: Calories: 303.4 | Protein: 4.5g |
Carbs: 19.4g | Fat: 23.6g | Fiber: 2.7g

Ingredients

- One tbsp. of oil
- One and a half tbsp. of butter
- One garlic clove (minced)
- Four shallots (chopped)
- Two red chili peppers (minced)
- One and a half tbsp. of lemongrass (chopped)
- Three cups of chicken stock
- Four cups of pumpkin (cubed)
- Two cups of coconut milk
- One bunch of basil leaves (chopped)

Method:

1. Take a medium-sized saucepan and add oil in it. Add the butter.

2. Start adding shallots, garlic, lemongrass, and chilies.

3. Add coconut milk, chicken stock, and pumpkin cubes. Boil the mixture.

4. Use a stick blender for blending the mixture into a smooth soup.

5. Serve hot with basil leaves.

Spicy Chicken Noodle Soup

Total Prep & Cooking Time: Eight hours and thirty minutes
Yields: Twelve servings
Nutrition Facts: Calories: 129.8 | Protein: 7.4g | Carbs: 15.4g | Fat: 2.9g | Fiber: 3.1g

Ingredients

- Five cups of chicken stock
- One cup of each
- White wine
- Water
- One onion (chopped)
- Three spring onions (chopped)
- Three garlic cloves (minced)
- Four carrots (cubed)
- Four celery stalks (chopped)
- Half tsp. of salt
- One tsp. of black pepper (ground)
- One tbsp. of curry powder
- Half tbsp. of each
- Sage (ground)
- Poultry seasoning
- Oregano (ground)
- One and a half tsp. of cayenne pepper
- Two tbsps. of oil
- Three chicken breasts (cut in strips)
- One red chili pepper (chopped)
- Twelve ounces of rice noodles

Method:

1. Cook the noodles by following the instructions on the packet. Keep aside.

2. Heat a slow cooker on low flame. Add white wine, chicken stock, spring onions, onion, carrots, garlic, salt, celery, curry powder, black pepper, cayenne pepper, poultry seasoning, and oregano.

3. Cook the chicken strips in an iron skillet.

4. Add the chicken strips to the slow cooker.

5. Keep cooking the soup for eight hours on low.

6. Add the red pepper along with the noodles fifteen minutes prior to serving.

7. Serve hot.

Thai Cucumber Soup

Total Prep & Cooking Time: One hour and five minutes
Yields: Six servings
Nutrition Facts: Calories: 113.4 | Protein: 2.6g | Carbs: 10.4g | Fat: 8.3g | Fiber: 1.6g

Ingredients

- Two tbsps. of butter
- Three tbsps. of onion (chopped)
- Three cucumbers (cubed)
- One-third cup of red wine vinegar
- One cup of chicken stock
- Two cups of water
- Three green chili peppers (chopped)
- Two and a half tbsp. of parsley (chopped)
- One tbsp. of each
- Cilantro (chopped)
- Lemongrass (chopped)
- Garlic (minced)
- Fish sauce
- Soy sauce
- One tsp. of ginger (ground)
- One pinch of salt
- Half cup of sour cream

Method:

1. Add the butter in a pan. Add onions and cook for two minutes.

2. Add vinegar, cucumbers, water, chicken stock, chili peppers, lemongrass, cilantro, parsley, fish sauce, garlic, ginger, and soy sauce. Simmer the mixture for twenty minutes.

3. Add the sour cream and simmer again for ten minutes.

4. Serve hot.

Khao Soi Soup

Total Prep & Cooking Time: One hour and fifteen minutes
Yields: Six servings
Nutrition Facts: Calories: 702.3 | Protein: 19.3g | Carbs: 56.2g | Fat: 47.8g | Fiber: 4.9g

Ingredients

- Six tbsps. of oil
- Three shallots (chopped)
- Three garlic cloves (minced)
- One-fourth cup of curry paste
- One tbsp. of curry powder
- Four cups of coconut milk
- Two cups of water
- Two and a half cup of chicken breast (cut in strips)
- One tsp. of salt
- One and a half tbsp. of each
- Fish sauce
- Sugar
- One-third tbsp. of lime juice
- Half cup of oil
- Twelve green chilies (chopped)
- Six shallots (chopped)
- Half head of bok choy
- Eight ounces of rice noodles
- One cup of pickled cabbage
- One-third cup of cilantro (chopped)
- One lime

Method:

1. Heat two tbsps. of oil in a steel wok. Add the garlic and shallots. Cook for four minutes. Add the curry paste along with the curry powder. Cook for two minutes. Add water, coconut milk, chicken strips, and salt. Boil the mixture. Simmer for ten minutes.

2. Add sugar, fish sauce, and lime juice. Stir well.

3. Add the remaining oil in an iron skillet and add the chili peppers. Cook for four minutes. Add the chili peppers to the soup.

4. Add shallots and bok choy in the skillet. Cook for four minutes. Add them to the soup.

5. Soak the noodles in hot water. Drain the water. Add the noodles to the skillet. Fry them for five minutes.

6. Serve the soup in soup bowls and top with pickled cabbage, lime wedges, cilantro, and fried noodles.

Sour Fish Soup (Tom Byoo)

Total Prep & Cooking Time: Fifty minutes
Yields: Four servings
Nutrition Facts: Calories: 170.6 | Protein: 17.3g |
Carbs: 12.9g | Fat: 5.1g | Fiber: 0.9g

Ingredients

- Three cups of fish stock
- One-inch piece of galangal root (chopped)
- Five green chilies (chopped)
- Two leaves of kaffir lime
- Two lemongrass stalks (chopped)
- Ten ounces of trout fish
- Five cherry tomatoes (halved)
- One-fourth cup of tamarind drink
- Two tbsps. of fish sauce
- One-fourth cup of cilantro (chopped)
- Two shallots (chopped)

Method:

1. Boil the fish stock in a large pot. Add galangal,
   chili peppers, lime leaves, shallots, and
   lemongrass. Simmer the mixture for twenty
   minutes.

2. Add fish, tamarind juice, tomatoes, and fish
   sauce. Simmer for five minutes.

3. Serve the soup hot. Garnish with chopped
   cilantro.

Thai Sirloin Salad

Total Prep & Cooking Time: Thirty minutes
Yields: Four servings
Nutrition Facts: Calories: 380.3 | Protein: 23.4g |
Carbs: 26.1g | Fat: 19.6g | Fiber: 6.9g

Ingredients

- Sixteen ounces of sirloin steak
- Five ounces of green lettuce and herb mix
- One ripe mango (sliced)
- One ripe avocado (sliced)
- Half cup of carrot (shredded)
- One cup of each
- Red bell pepper (diced)
- Yellow bell pepper
- Half tsp. of salt
- Two tbsps. of peanuts (roasted)

For the dressing:

- Three tbsps. of honey
- Two and a half tbsp. of peanut butter
- Four tbsps. of hot water
- One tbsp. of each
- White vinegar
- Soy sauce
- Sesame oil

Method:

1. Grill the steak for fifteen minutes. Flip in between.

2. Whisk all the ingredients for the dressing in a bowl. Mix well.

3. Arrange the lettuce mix on a dish along with avocado, mango, bell pepper, and carrot on top of lettuce.

4. Slice the steak and season with some salt. Add the steak over the salad.

5. Drizzle the prepared seasoning from the top and sprinkle the peanuts.

6. Serve immediately.

Thai-Style Cucumber Salad

Total Prep & Cooking Time: Forty-five minutes
Yields: Four servings
Nutrition Facts: Calories: 227.3 | Protein: 5.7g |
Carbs: 34.3g | Fat: 9.2g | Fiber: 2.9g

Ingredients

- Three cucumbers (cut in slices of one-fourth inch)
- One tbsp. of salt
- Half cup of each
- Rice wine vinegar
- White sugar
- Peanuts (chopped)
- Two jalapeno peppers (chopped)
- One-fourth cup of cilantro (chopped)

Method:

1. Toss the slices of cucumber in a colander with some salt. Leave the colander in the sink for draining all the water for thirty minutes.

2. Rinse the cucumber slices with cold water. Dry using paper towels.

3. Combine vinegar and sugar in a bowl. Add jalapeno peppers, cucumber slices, and cilantro.

4. Toss for combining the ingredients.

5. Serve by sprinkling chopped peanuts on the top.

Thai Shrimp Salad

Total Prep & Cooking Time: One hour and thirty minutes
Yields: Six servings
Nutrition Facts: Calories: 210.3| Protein: 23.6g | Carbs: 15.2g | Fat: 3.3g | Fiber: 0.6g

Ingredients

- Two cups of water
- Half cup of salt
- One-third cup of sugar
- One-fourth cup of soy sauce
- Two pounds of jumbo shrimps (deveined, peeled)
- Two tbsps. of lemon juice
- One tbsp. of sesame oil
- Half tsp. of cayenne pepper
- One and a half tbsp. of garlic (minced)
- One cup of peppers (sliced, yellow, orange, red)
- Two and a half tbsp. of cilantro (chopped)

Method:

1. For brining the shrimps, mix salt, water, soy sauce, and sugar in a bowl. Add the prawns. Brine for about one hour.

2. Preheat your oven at two-hundred degrees Celsius.

3. Rinse the shrimps and arrange them on a baking tray. Roast for eight minutes.

4. Combine soy sauce, lemon juice, cayenne pepper, sesame oil, and garlic in a mixing bowl. Add the shrimps, cilantro, and peppers.

5. Toss for combining.

**Tangy Cabbage Salad**

Total Prep & Cooking Time: One hour and thirty minutes
Yields: Six servings
Nutrition Facts: Calories: 130.2 | Protein: 5.3g | Carbs: 13.6g | Fat: 6.5g | Fiber: 4.6g

Ingredients

- Two limes
- One tbsp. of each
- Chili paste
- Sugar
- Vegetable oil
- One small head cabbage (chopped)
- Two carrots (chopped)
- One small red bell pepper (diced)
- Half cucumber (cubed)
- One-third cup of cilantro (chopped)
- Half cup of peanuts (roasted)
- One pinch of salt

Method:

1. Combine the chili paste, sugar, and lime juice in a small-sized bowl. Add the oil slowly and combine it.

2. Combine cabbage, bell pepper, carrots, cilantro, cucumber, and peanuts in a mixing bowl. Add pepper and salt.

3. Pour the prepared dressing over the mixed veggies. Toss for coating.

4. Chill the salad for thirty minutes.

Thai Salmon Salad

Total Prep & Cooking Time: Fifty-five minutes
Yields: Six servings
Nutrition Facts: Calories: 240.3 | Protein: 24.6g |
Carbs: 10.6g | Fat: 9.6g | Fiber: 2.9g

Ingredients

- Four tbsps. of each
- Fish sauce
- Lime juice
- Two tsps. of sugar
- Four green chilies (chopped)
- Two pounds of salmon
- One tsp. of olive oil
- One onion (chopped)
- One tomato (chopped)
- One cup of basil (chopped)
- One head of lettuce

Method:

1. Preheat your oven at two-hundred degrees Celsius.

2. Combine lime juice, fish sauce, chilies, and brown sugar. Mix well.

3. Arrange the fillets of salmon on a baking sheet and rub with some olive oil. Bake for twenty minutes.

4. Add the baked fillets of salmon in a large bowl. Break the fillets using a fork into bite-size chunks. Add basil, tomato, and onion. Add the dressing and toss.

5. Arrange the salmon mixture on lettuce leaves.

Thai Grapefruit, Coconut, Chicken, and Shrimp Salad

Total Prep & Cooking Time: Thirty minutes
Yields: Six servings
Nutrition Facts: Calories: 359.3 | Protein: 29.6g |
Carbs: 24.6g | Fat: 15.6g | Fiber: 6.6g

Ingredients

- Half cup of lime juice
- Two tbsps. of fish sauce
- Two tsps. of each
- Garlic (minced)
- Sugar
- One grapefruit (chopped)
- Two cups of shrimp (cooked)
- Two and a half cup of chicken breast (cooked, cut in strips
- One and a half cup of coconut meat (chopped)
- Six shallots (chopped)
- One tsp. of green chili pepper
- One-third cup of mint leaves
- Three-fourth tbsp. of cilantro (chopped)
- One head of iceberg lettuce (shredded)

Method:

1. Combine fish sauce, lime juice, garlic, and sugar.

2. Toss together shrimp, grapefruit, coconut, strips of chicken, chili pepper, shallots,

cilantro, and mint in a bowl. Add three-fourth of the dressing. Toss for combining.

3. Toss the lettuce with the remaining dressing.

4. Arrange the lettuce on a dish. Top with grapefruit mixture. Serve immediately.

Chapter 7: Tofu Recipes

Tofu forms an integral part of both vegetarian and non-vegetarian recipes. The simple flavor of tofu can help in uplifting the extra-ordinary taste of Thai cuisine. Here are some Thai tofu recipes for you that can be made easily at your home kitchen.

<u>*Thai Tofu*</u>

Total Prep & Cooking Time: Thirty minutes
Yields: Six servings
Nutrition Facts: Calories: 280.6 | Protein: 19.6g | Carbs: 9.5g | Fat: 18.2g | Fiber: 4.1g

Ingredients

- Fourteen ounces of tofu (firm, cubed)
- One-third cup of spring onion (chopped)
- Two tsps. of olive oil
- Half tsp. of sesame oil
- One tsp. of soy sauce
- Two and a half tsp. of ginger root (grated)
- One-fourth cup of peanut butter (chunky)
- Three tbsps. of coconut meat (chopped)
- One-third tsp. of sesame seeds

Method:

1. Heat sesame oil along with olive oil in an iron skillet. Add the spring onions. Cook for one minute.

2. Add the cubes of tofu and cook for four minutes. Add the soy sauce. Add the ginger and peanut butter. Stir for combining.

3. Remove the skillet from heat. Add the coconut meat. Toss for combining.

4. Serve with sesame seed garnishing.

Tofu Pad Thai

Total Prep & Cooking Time: Forty-five minutes
Yields: Four servings
Nutrition Facts: Calories: 412.3 | Protein: 13.4g |
Carbs: 59.6g | Fat: 15.2g | Fiber: 3.2g

Ingredients

- Twelve ounces of tofu (cubed)
- One tbsp. of cornstarch
- Three tbsps. of oil
- Eight ounces of rice noodles

For the sauce:

- One-fourth cup of each
- Water
- Sriracha sauce
- Soy sauce
- Two tbsps. of sugar
- One tbsp. of each
- Tamarind concentrate
- Peanuts (roasted)
- One tsp. of red pepper flakes
- Half onion (chopped)
- One large egg
- Two and a half tbsp. of spring onion (chopped)
- One lime

Method:

1. Start by coating the tofu cubes in cornstarch in a large bowl.

2. Add two tbsps. of oil in a steel wok. Add the tofu cubes and cook for two minutes on each side.

3. Add the noodles in a bowl. Pour boiling water over the noodles. Soak them for three minutes. Drain the water.

4. Mix sriracha, water, sugar, tamarind concentrate, soy sauce, and red pepper flakes in a pan. Stir the sauce and cook for five minutes.

5. Add one tbsp. of oil in a large wok. Add noodles, chopped onion, and tofu. Cook for three minutes.

6. Add the sauce gradually and toss to combine.

7. Push the mixture of noodles to one side and crack the egg in the middle. Cook the egg for eight minutes and mix it with the noodles.

8. Garnish the noodles with peanuts, lime wedges, and spring onions.

Thai-Style Stuffed Tofu

Total Prep & Cooking Time: One hour and five minutes
Yields: Four servings
Nutrition Facts: Calories: 370.2 | Protein: 20.3g | Carbs: 21.3g | Fat: 23.6g | Fiber: 3.9g

Ingredients

- Twenty-four ounces of tofu (extra firm)
- One-fourth cup of shiitake mushrooms
- One zucchini (chopped)
- One onion (halved)
- Three garlic cloves (minced)
- One jalapeno pepper (chopped)
- One large egg
- Two tbsps. of soy sauce
- Two and a half tbsp. of ginger (minced)
- One tbsp. of hoisin sauce
- One and a half tbsp. of cornstarch
- One cup of each
- Vegetable oil
- Cabbage (shredded)

Method:

1. Drain the tofu and cut them into squares of four-inch. Cut the squares into two triangles diagonally. Keep aside.

2. Add the mushrooms in hot water and let them rehydrate until plump and moist. Soak for

twenty minutes. Cut the stems and chop the mushrooms.

3. Add onion, zucchini, jalapeno pepper, and garlic in a food processor. Blend until the veggies form a paste. Transfer the paste to a large bowl.

4. Add egg, mushrooms, ginger, soy sauce, hoisin sauce, and cornstarch. Add the shredded cabbage and mix.

5. Add two tbsps. of oil in a skillet. Add the tofu triangles and cook for two minutes on each side. Let the tofu cool down.

6. Use a sharp knife for cutting a slit on one side of the tofu and scoop out the center. Fill the center with the stuffing.

7. Heat two tbsps. of oil in an iron skillet and add the stuffed tofu. Place the stuffed-side down. Cook for five minutes.

8. Serve hot.

Thai Tofu Curry

Total Prep & Cooking Time: Forty-five minutes
Yields: Four servings
Nutrition Facts: Calories: 279.3 | Protein: 9.6g |
Carbs: 7.2g | Fat: 24.6g | Fiber: 2.9g

Ingredients

- One tbsp. of vegetable oil
- Twelve ounces of tofu (extra firm)
- One and a half tbsp. of each
- Seasoned salt
- Butter
- One small onion (chopped)
- Three garlic cloves (minced)
- One can of coconut milk
- Two tsps. of curry powder
- Half tsp. of salt
- One-fourth tsp. of black pepper (ground)
- One-third cup of cilantro (chopped)

Method:

1. Heat some oil in an iron skillet. Add the cubes of tofu and add seasoned salt. Cook for fifteen minutes. Keep aside.

2. Melt the butter in the skillet. Add the garlic. Add the onions and cook for two minutes.

3. Add the coconut milk, pepper, salt, curry powder, and cilantro. Add the tofu cubes and mix well. Simmer for fifteen minutes.

4. Serve hot with rice.

Thai-Style Baked Tofu

Total Prep & Cooking Time: One hour and fifteen minutes
Yields: Two servings
Nutrition Facts: Calories: 329.3 | Protein: 19.2g | Carbs: 22.6g | Fat: 18.9g | Fiber: 2.9g

Ingredients

- One pound of tofu
- Two tbsps. of each
- Agave nectar
- Sesame oil
- Soy sauce
- One tsp. of each
- Ginger root (minced)
- Garlic (minced)
- One tbsp. of sesame seeds

Method:

1. Start by preheating your oven at one-hundred and seventy-five degrees Celsius. Use some oil for greasing a baking tray.

2. Press the tofu for discarding excess water. Arrange the pieces of tofu on the greased baking tray.

3. Mix agave nectar, soy sauce, garlic, sesame oil, and ginger in a bowl.

4. Brush the prepared marinade over the pieces of tofu.

5. Bake the tofu for thirty minutes. Flip the pieces of tofu and brush with the remaining marinade. Sprinkle the sesame seeds over the tofu. Bake for thirty minutes.

6. Serve warm.

Tofu Spring Rolls

Total Prep & Cooking Time: Fifty minutes
Yields: Twelve servings
Nutrition Facts: Calories: 72.3 | Protein: 6.3 | Carbs: 11.2 | Fat: 2.1 | Fiber: 3.6g

Ingredients

For the sauce:

- Two tbsps. of each
- Fish sauce
- Soy sauce
- Lime juice
- One-fourth tsp. of sugar

For the spring rolls:

- Two tbsps. of oil
- Three garlic cloves (minced)
- One-inch piece of galangal (grated)
- Two green onions (sliced in matchsticks)
- One red chili (minced)
- Half cup of cabbage (chopped)
- Six shiitake mushrooms (cut in matchsticks)
- One-third cup of tofu (cut in matchsticks)
- Two cups of bean sprouts
- Twelve wrappers for spring roll
- Three-fourth cup of cilantro (chopped)
- One cup of basil (chopped)

Method:

1. Combine the sauce ingredients in a bowl. Mix well for dissolving the sugar.

2. Add two tbsps. of oil in a steel wok. Add galangal, garlic, chili, and green onion. Cook for one minute.

3. Add mushrooms, tofu, and cabbage. Stir-fry for two minutes. Add the sauce and cook for two minutes.

4. Remove the wok from heat and mix the bean sprouts.

5. For assembling the rolls, lay the roll wrappers on a flat surface and place one tbsp. of the stuffing in the middle. Spread the stuffing.

6. Sprinkle basil and cilantro over the stuffing. Roll the wrappers and tuck in the ends.

7. Add one-inch of frying oil in a wok. Add the spring rolls and fry them for one minute on each side.

8. Drain excess oil.

9. Cut from the center and serve hot.

Thai Garlic and Black Pepper Tofu

Total Prep & Cooking Time: One hour and five minutes
Yields: Four servings
Nutrition Facts: Calories: 170.3 | Protein: 14.2g | Carbs: 19.1g | Fat: 6.3g | Fiber: 5.9g

Ingredients

For the tofu and seasoning:

- Fourteen ounces of tofu (extra firm)
- One tbsp. of soy sauce
- Two tbsps. of each
- Garlic cloves (minced)
- Water
- One tsp. of black pepper (ground)
- Half tsp. of rice vinegar

For the vegetables:

- One small onion (sliced in wedges)
- One red bell pepper (sliced)
- Six garlic cloves (minced)
- Three ounces of shiitake mushrooms (sliced)
- Eight ounces of kale (leaves sliced)
- One bunch of asparagus (trimmed, cut in pieces of one-inch)

For the sauce:

- Two tbsps. of soy sauce
- Half cup of vegetable stock
- One tsp. of sriracha sauce
- One and a half tsp. of black pepper (ground)
- Two tsps. of cornstarch

Method:

1. Start by cutting the tofu into slices of half-inch. Remove the excess moisture by pressing the slices.

2. Mix the ingredients for the tofu seasoning in a bowl. Add the tofu slices and coat them in the seasoning.

3. Preheat your oven at two-hundred degrees Celsius. Use parchment paper for lining a baking tray. Arrange the tofu slices on the tray and bake for fifteen minutes. Flip the slices and bake for fifteen minutes.

4. Chop the veggies. Combine the ingredients for the sauce in a mixing bowl.

5. Grease a wok with some oil and add half a cup of water. Add the chopped onions and cook for two minutes.

6. Add garlic, mushrooms, and bell pepper. Add the kale. Mix well and cover the wok.

7. Add the asparagus along with the sauce. Cook for two minutes.

8. Arrange the vegetables on serving plates. Top with tofu slices.

9. Serve hot.

Thai Tofu and Coconut Curry

Total Prep & Cooking Time: Thirty minutes
Yields: Six servings
Nutrition Facts: Calories: 239.3 | Protein: 5.6g |
Carbs: 7.3g | Fat: 20.6g | Fiber: 1.6g

Ingredients

- Twelve ounces of tofu (extra firm, cut in cubes)
- Three tbsps. of avocado oil
- Two tbsps. of red curry paste
- Fourteen ounces of coconut milk
- One tbsp. of soy sauce
- One and a half tbsp. of coconut sugar
- Half lime (juiced)
- One tsp. of paprika

Method:

1. Heat oil in a large pan. Add the cubes of tofu. Cook for three minutes on each side.

2. Heat another saucepan. Add the red curry paste. Cook for thirty seconds and add the coconut milk. Mix well.

3. Boil the mixture for four minutes. Add soy sauce, lime juice, coconut sugar, and paprika. Add the cooked tofu cubes and mix well.

4. Serve hot with rice.

Tofu and Thai-Style Peanut Sauce

Total Prep & Cooking Time: Forty minutes
Yields: Two servings
Nutrition Facts: Calories: 210.3 | Protein: 11.5g |
Carbs: 9.7g | Fat: 12.7g | Fiber: 1.9g

Ingredients

For the sauce:

- Two tbsps. of each
- Coconut oil
- Brown sugar
- Soy sauce
- One tsp. of each
- Ginger (grated)
- Green chili (minced)
- One garlic clove (minced)
- One lime (half juiced and half zest)
- Two tsps. of red curry paste
- One cup of vegetable stock
- Half cup of each
- Coconut milk
- Peanut butter

For the tofu:

- Fourteen ounces of tofu (firm)
- Two tbsps. of coconut oil
- One pound of spinach (rinsed)
- Salt (for seasoning)

Method:

1. Add two tbsps. of coconut oil in a saucepan. Add chili, ginger, lime zest, garlic, and curry paste. Cook the mixture for two minutes.

2. Add peanut butter, vegetable stock, brown sugar, coconut milk, and soy sauce. Mix well. Boil the mixture and simmer for five minutes. Remove the pan from heat and add lime juice.

3. Remove excess liquid from the tofu. Cut the tofu into cubes.

4. Add two tbsps. of oil in an iron skillet. Add the tofu cubes and cook for two minutes. Use salt for seasoning.

5. Boil the spinach leaves for two minutes. Drain the water.

6. Transfer tofu cubes and cooked spinach on a plate. Top with the prepared peanut sauce.

Spicy Tofu With Peanuts and Red Bell Pepper

Total Prep & Cooking Time: Twenty minutes
Yields: Four servings
Nutrition Facts: Calories: 365.3 | Protein: 14.2g |
Carbs: 12.3g | Fat: 24.6g | Fiber: 5.9g

Ingredients

- One-third cup of olive oil
- Two red bell peppers (sliced)
- Three tbsps. of ginger (grated)
- Four garlic cloves (minced)
- Fourteen ounces of tofu (extra firm, cut in cubes of one-inch)
- Three green onions (sliced)
- Three and a half tbsp. of soy sauce
- Two tbsps. of lime juice
- Three-fourth tsp. of red pepper flakes
- Six ounces of spinach leaves
- One cup of basil (chopped)
- One-fourth cup of peanuts (roasted)

Method:

1. Add oil in a steel wok. Add ginger, bell peppers, and garlic. Sauté for two minutes.

2. Add green onions and tofu. Stir-fry for two minutes.

3. Add soy sauce, pepper flakes, and lime juice. Mix well.

4. Add the spinach leaves and cook for one minute. Add pepper and salt for seasoning.

5. Sprinkle basil from the top. Toss for combining.

6. Garnish with peanuts. Serve hot.

Crispy Tofu Panang Curry

Total Prep & Cooking Time: Forty-five minutes
Yields: Six servings
Nutrition Facts: Calories: 269.3 | Protein: 9.3g |
Carbs: 12.3g | Fat: 22.6g | Fiber: 2.2g

Ingredients

- One pound of tofu (extra firm)
- Two tbsps. of coconut oil
- One onion (chopped)
- Three bell peppers (red, yellow, green, chopped)
- Two garlic cloves (minced)
- Four ounces of Panang curry paste
- One tbsp. of peanut butter
- Twelve leaves of kaffir lime (crushed)
- Fourteen ounces of coconut milk
- Three tbsps. of fish sauce
- One-fourth cup of basil leaves (chopped)

Method:

1. Preheat your oven at one-hundred and seventy-five degrees Celsius.

2. Squeeze out excess moisture from the tofu.

3. Cut the tofu in cubes of half an inch. Add salt and mix well.

4. Add oil in an iron skillet. Add the cubes of tofu. Sauté the tofu for five minutes.

5. Arrange the cubes on a baking tray. Bake them for fifteen minutes in the oven.

6. Chop peppers and onions.

7. Heat a skillet and add coconut oil. Add onions, garlic, and peppers. Cook for three minutes.

8. Push the veggies to one side. Add the curry paste. Add fish sauce, lime leaves, and coconut milk. Mix the veggies.

9. Simmer the mixture for ten minutes. Add the tofu cubes.

10. Remove from heat and garnish with basil leaves.

Thai-Style Tofu Collard Wraps

Total Prep & Cooking Time: Thirty minutes
Yields: Six servings
Nutrition Facts: Calories: 265.3 | Protein: 12.3g |
Carbs: 12.1g | Fat: 22.8g | Fiber: 2.6g

Ingredients

For the wraps:

- Six leaves of collard green
- Two tbsps. of soy sauce
- One tsp. of garlic powder
- Half tsp. of red pepper flakes
- Sixteen ounces of tofu (extra firm, cut in strips of half-inch)
- One tbsp. of sesame oil
- One cucumber (julienned)
- One carrot (shredded)
- Two and a half tbsp. of each
- Scallions (sliced)
- Mint leaves
- Basil leaves (chopped)

For the sauce:

- Half cup of peanut butter
- One tbsp. of sriracha
- Four tsps. of sesame oil
- One and a half tbsp. of honey
- Two tbsps. of lime juice

- Three tbsps. of water
- Salt (for seasoning)

Method:

1. Start by preparing the collard leaves. Cut the stems and remove the thick area of the stem using a sharp knife. Blanch the leaves in hot water for one minute.

2. Submerge the collard leaves in an ice bath for two minutes.

3. Combine sesame oil, peanut butter, sriracha, lime juice, honey, salt, and water. Mix well.

4. Take another small bowl and mix garlic powder, soy sauce, and pepper flakes. Add this mixture over the strips of tofu. Marinate for fifteen minutes.

5. Take a pan and heat oil in it. Cook the strips of tofu for two minutes on all sides.

6. For arranging the wrap, lay flat the collard leaves on a working surface. Add two tsps. of peanut sauce and spread it out evenly. Add one strip of tofu along with four pieces of cucumber, mint, one tbsp. of carrot, scallions, and basil.

7. Fold the leaves.

8. Serve the wraps with a bit of sauce over the wraps.

Thai Quinoa-Tofu Bowl

Total Prep & Cooking Time: One hour
Yields: Four servings
Nutrition Facts: Calories: 329.3 | Protein: 18.2g |
Carbs: 32.6g | Fat: 12.5g | Fiber: 7.3g

Ingredients

- Three-hundred and fifty grams of tofu (extra firm)
- Three-fourth cup of quinoa (rinsed)
- Two tbsps. of lime juice
- Two and a half tbsp. of peanut butter
- One tbsp. of water
- Half tbsp. of soy sauce
- Two tsps. of honey
- Two and a half tsp. of ginger (grated)
- One garlic clove (minced)
- Half tsp. of red chili flakes
- Two carrots (grated)
- One cup of each
- Edamame
- Red cabbage (sliced)
- One green onion (sliced)
- Half cup of cilantro (chopped)
- Four tsps. of sesame seeds (toasted)

Method:

1. Preheat your oven at two-hundred degrees Celsius. Use aluminum foil for lining a baking tray. Spray the foil with some oil.

2. Cut the tofu into cubes of three-fourth inch. Arrange the cubes on the tray and bake for twenty minutes.

3. Cook the quinoa according to the packet instructions.

4. Combine together water, lime juice, peanut butter, honey, tamari, garlic, chili flakes, and ginger in a bowl.

5. Combine carrots with the quinoa. Add edamame, cilantro, cabbage, green onion, and sesame seeds. Mix well.

6. Add the tofu along with the dressing.

7. Toss for combining.

Thai Tofu and Ginger Mushrooms

Total Prep & Cooking Time: Forty minutes
Yields: Four servings
Nutrition Facts: Calories: 475.6 | Protein: 28.6 g |
Carbs: 71.3g | Fat: 13.5g | Fiber: 6.2g

Ingredients

- Two cups of jasmine rice
- Two mushrooms
- Two red onions
- One-inch ginger (grated)
- Two red chilies (minced)
- Sixteen ounces of tofu
- Two zucchini
- Two carrots
- Three garlic cloves (minced)
- One bunch of cilantro (chopped)
- Six cups of water
- One tbsp. of rice wine vinegar
- Two tsps. of vegetable oil
- Four tbsps. of soy sauce
- One and a half tsp. of sugar

Method:

1. Start by cutting the tofu into small cubes. Cut the zucchini in thick slices. Slice the mushrooms along with the onions. Shred the carrots, or you can julienne them as well.

2. Boil the jasmine rice in a pot for ten minutes. Drain the water.

3. Combine rice wine vinegar, soy sauce, and sugar in a bowl.

4. Add oil in a steel wok. Add the cubes of tofu. Cook for two minutes. Add zucchini, mushrooms, carrot, and onions. Cook for four minutes.

5. Add red chili, garlic, and ginger. Add the mixture of soy sauce and cook for one minute.

6. Add the cilantro and toss for two minutes.

7. Serve hot.

Steamed Tofu in Banana Leaf

Total Prep & Cooking Time: Thirty minutes
Yields: Four servings
Nutrition Facts: Calories: 65.3 | Protein: 4.2g | Carbs:
2.3g | Fat: 3.5g | Fiber: 0.9g

Ingredients

- Fourteen ounces of tofu (firm)
- Two stalks of lemongrass (chopped)
- Two leaves of lime
- Two tsps. of galangal (grated)
- Two Thai chilies (chopped)
- Half cup of basil (chopped)
- One lime
- Banana leaves

Method:

1. Remove excess moisture from the tofu.

2. Cut the banana leaves according to the required size. Add one cube of tofu in each leaf along with the herbs.

3. Wrap the banana leaves and secure with a toothpick.

4. Steam the banana leaves for ten minutes.

Stir-Fried Tofu With Eggplant and Basil

Total Prep & Cooking Time: Thirty minutes
Yields: Four servings
Nutrition Facts: Calories: 260.3 | Protein: 11.2g |
Carbs: 34.6g | Fat: 9.2g | Fiber: 12.3g

Ingredients

- One tbsp. of oil
- Two cups of tofu (firm, cut in cubes on one-inch)
- One and a half tbsp. of red chili (minced)
- Five garlic cloves (minced)
- Three cups of eggplant (cut in rounds of one-inch, quartered)
- One cup of red bell pepper (cut in chunks)
- Half cup of basil leaves

For the sauce:

- Two tbsps. of each
- Soy sauce
- Water
- Two tsps. of sugar
- One tbsp. of sesame oil

Method:

1. Prepare the sauce by mixing all the listed ingredients.

2. Heat some oil in an iron skillet.

3. Add the tofu along with red chili. Cook the mixture for five minutes.

4. Add the garlic. Cook for two minutes.

5. Add red peppers, eggplant, and basil. Add the sauce and toss to combine.

6. Cook the mixture for two minutes.

7. Garnish with basil. Serve warm.

Tofu Pad Krapow Moo

Total Prep & Cooking Time: Thirty minutes
Yields: Four servings
Nutrition Facts: Calories: 560.3 | Protein: 41.2g |
Carbs: 75.8g | Fat: 24.6g | Fiber: 8.6g

Ingredients

- Two cups of rice
- Two red onions
- Two tbsps. of garlic (minced)
- Half tbsp. of brown sugar
- One bunch of basil
- One-hundred grams of green beans
- One red chili (chopped)
- One lime
- Four tbsps. of ginger (grated)
- Two tsps. of soy sauce
- Three-hundred grams of tofu
- Five tbsps. of oil
- Pepper and salt (for seasoning)

Method:

1. Add the rice in a pot. Add two cups of water.
   Boil the rice for twelve minutes.

2. Remove excess moisture from the tofu.

3. Mash the tofu into small pieces. Add pepper
   and salt.

4. Cut the stems of the green beans and cut them in half.

5. Use half of the lemon for making zest and half for juice.

6. Take a large pan. Add one tbsp. of oil. Add onions and green beans. Use pepper for seasoning.

7. Add garlic, ginger, and chili. Cook for one minute.

8. Add the tofu. Mix well and cook for six minutes.

9. Add brown sugar along with soy sauce. Cook for two minutes. Add lime zest and one tbsp. of water. Cook for one minute.

10. Use fork for fluffing the cooked rice. Add salt for seasoning.

11. Arrange the rice on serving plates. Top with the mixture of tofu.

12. Garnish with basil leaves.

Chapter 8: Snacks & Dessert Recipes

After some lip-smacking Thai main course, you can easily surprise your guests and friends with a simple Thai snack along with a tasty dessert right at the end. In this section, you will find various Thai snack and dessert recipes - superb when paired with something else or served on their own.

Thai-Style Mini Lettuce Shrimp Wraps

Total Prep & Cooking Time: Thirty minutes
Yields: Six servings
Nutrition Facts: Calories: 324.1 | Protein: 27.6g | Carbs: 14.2g | Fat: 16.8g | Fiber: 4.6g

Ingredients

- One-third cup of unsweetened coconut (shredded)
- One cup of baby shrimp
- One-fourth cup of peanuts (roasted, chopped)
- Two green onions (sliced)
- Two garlic cloves (minced)
- Two tsps. of galangal (grated)
- One red chili (minced)
- Half tsp. of chili powder
- Three-fourth tsp. of sugar
- One tbsp. of fish sauce
- Three tbsps. of coconut milk
- One head of romaine lettuce

- Half cup of coriander
- One lime (sliced in wedges)

Method:

1. Add the shredded coconut in a wok. Fry the coconut for two minutes. Keep aside.

2. Place the baby shrimps in a bowl. Add the peanuts. Mix well and add garlic, spring onion, chili, galangal, chili powder, fish sauce, and sugar. Toss the ingredients for mixing.

3. Add the coconut milk. Stir for combining.

4. Add the toasted shredded coconut.

5. The taste needs to be salt, sweet, sour, and spicy.

6. For assembling, cut the tops of the lettuce leaves. Lay them flat on a dish. Add one tbsp. of the shrimp mixture on the center of each leaf. Sprinkle coriander over the wraps.

7. For serving, squeeze some lemon juice from the top. Wrap up and eat in one go.

Crispy Pork Ribs and Thai Marinade

Total Prep & Cooking Time: Thirty minutes
Yields: Four servings
Nutrition Facts: Calories: 556.3 | Protein: 50.3g |
Carbs: 24.9g | Fat: 24.6g | Fiber: 3.5g

Ingredients

- Two pounds of pork ribs (chopped into three segments)
- Eight garlic cloves (minced)
- Three-fourth cup of coriander (chopped)
- Two tbsps. of fish sauce
- One tbsp. of sherry
- Half cup of flour
- One-third tsp. of salt
- One-fourth tsp. of black pepper (ground)
- Two cups of oil

Method:

1. Add coriander, garlic, sherry, and fish sauce in a blender. Blend for making aromatic Thai green marinade.

2. Add the pork ribs in a bowl and pour over the marinade. Toss for combining. Let the pork ribs rest in the refrigerator for twenty minutes.

3. Mix flour with pepper and salt in a bowl. Coat the marinated ribs in the flour mixture.

4. Heat the oil in a steel wok. Add the pork ribs. Cook for six minutes on each side.

5. Serve the rib shot with a dipping sauce of your choice.

Chicken Satay

Total Prep & Cooking Time: Forty minutes
Yields: Four servings
Nutrition Facts: Calories: 441.3 | Protein: 32.3g |
Carbs: 24.9g | Fat: 21.3g | Fiber: 1.8g

Ingredients

- One pound of chicken thigh (boneless, cut in bite-size strips)
- Two tbsps. of lemongrass (minced)
- Five garlic cloves (minced)
- One tsp. of galangal (grated)
- One-fourth cup of cilantro (chopped)
- Two tsps. of each
- Cumin (ground)
- Coriander (ground)
- Half tsp. of turmeric
- One-third tsp. of white pepper (ground)
- One red chili (minced)
- Four tbsps. of fish sauce
- Three tsps. of brown sugar
- Half tbsp. of rice vinegar
- One and a half tbsp. of each
- Vegetable oil
- Honey

Method:

1. Add all the ingredients in a blender except for the chicken strips. Blend for making a smooth satay marinade.

2. Pour the prepared marinade over the chicken strips. Mix well. Marinate the chicken strips for thirty minutes.

3. Soak twelve satay sticks in water to prevent burning the sticks.

4. Thread the marinated chicken strips into the skewers.

5. Heat a grill pan. Brush the pan with some oil.

6. Add the satay sticks. Cook the chicken satay for fifteen minutes. Flip in between and baste with the remaining marinade.

7. Serve hot.

Thai Fried Calamari

Total Prep & Cooking Time: Thirty minutes
Yields: Four servings
Nutrition Facts: Calories: 456.9 | Protein: 31.2g |
Carbs: 59.6g | Fat: 12.3g | Fiber: 4.7g

Ingredients

- Two large tubes of squid
- Half cup of semolina
- Half tsp. of salt
- One-eighth tsp. of cayenne pepper
- One-third tsp. of five-spice powder
- One pinch of black pepper (ground)
- One cup of canola oil

Method:

1. Add semolina flour in a bowl. Add spices and salt. Mix well.

2. Place the squid tubes on a cutting board. Use a sharp knife for slicing the tubes half-inch wide. You will need to make squid rings from the tubes.

3. Roll the squid rings in the mixture of flour. Keep aside.

4. Add oil in a pan. Add the squid rings and fry for five minutes.

5. Drain excess oil by placing the squid rings on paper towels.

6. Serve hot.

Corn Fritters

Total Prep & Cooking Time: Twenty minutes
Yields: Twelve servings
Nutrition Facts: Calories: 197.6 | Protein: 4.5g |
Carbs: 8.2g | Fat: 16.7g | Fiber: 1.6g

Ingredients

- One cup of rice flour
- One tsp. of baking powder
- Two tbsps. of fish sauce
- Two and a half tbsp. of soy sauce
- Two large eggs
- Half block of tofu (firm, cut in small cubes)
- One and a half cup of corn
- Four green onions (chopped)
- Half cup of coriander (chopped)
- Half bell pepper (diced)
- One green chili (minced)
- One-third tsp. of turmeric
- One cup of canola oil (for frying)

Method:

1. Crack the eggs in a large bowl. Add salt, fish sauce, and soy sauce. Whisk well.

2. Add corn, tofu, coriander, green onion, chili, bell pepper, and turmeric. Combine the ingredients.

3. Combine flour along with baking powder in a bowl. Add this mixture slowly to the egg mixture. Stir for making a thick mixture.

4. Heat canola oil in a frying pan. Add one tbsp. of the mixture into the hot oil. Fry the fritters for two minutes on each side.

5. Drain excess oil by placing the fritters on paper towels.

6. Serve the fritters hot with any dipping sauce of your choice.

Thai Coconut Shrimp

Total Prep & Cooking Time: Thirty minutes
Yields: Four servings
Nutrition Facts: Calories: 160.2 | Protein: 9.1g |
Carbs: 12.3g | Fat: 7.9g | Fiber: 2.6g

Ingredients

- Eighteen medium-sized shrimps
- Half cup of shredded coconut (unsweetened)
- Three eggs

For the coating mix:

- One cup of panko bread crumbs
- Half tsp. of salt
- One tsp. of onion powder
- One-third tsp. of garlic powder
- One-eighth tsp. of cayenne pepper

Method:

1. Preheat your oven at one-hundred and seventy-five degrees Celsius. Use cooking spray for greasing a baking sheet.

2. Combine the ingredients for the coating mix in a bowl.

3. In another bowl, beat the eggs.

4. Place the coconut in another bowl.

5. Hold the shrimps by the tails and dip them in the eggs. Coat the shrimps in coating mix and then dip them back in the egg. Roll the shrimps in the shredded coconut.

6. Arrange the shrimps on the greased baking sheet.

7. Bake for twenty minutes. Flip the shrimps in the middle.

8. Serve hot.

Seared Scallops and Thai Sauce

Total Prep & Cooking Time: Twenty minutes
Yields: Four servings
Nutrition Facts: Calories: 154.6 | Protein: 9.1g | Carbs: 25.9g | Fat: 2.6g | Fiber: 3.2g

Ingredients

- Ten scallops
- Two tbsps. of oil
- One pinch of pepper and salt

For the sauce:

- Three tbsps. of oil
- One tbsp. of fish sauce
- Half lime (juiced)
- One red chili (minced)
- One-fourth tsp. of cayenne pepper
- Two garlic cloves (minced)
- One and a half tbsp. of coconut milk

Method:

1. Rinse the scallops. Pat dry the scallops using paper towels.

2. Add two tbsps. of oil in a frying pan. Place the scallops on the hot oil and sear for two minutes on each side. Season with pepper and salt.

3. Remove excess oil from the scallops by placing them on paper towels.

4. Add all the listed ingredients for the sauce in a pan. Mix well and warm the sauce for two minutes.

5. Arrange the scallops on serving plates. Spoon the prepared Thai sauce all over the seared scallops.

6. Serve immediately.

Baked Chili-Garlic Shrimp

Total Prep & Cooking Time: Thirty minutes
Yields: Two servings
Nutrition Facts: Calories: 240.3 | Protein: 21.2g |
Carbs: 2.4g | Fat: 2.6g | Fiber: 0.9g

Ingredients

- Twenty medium-sized shrimps
- Two tbsps. of vegetable oil
- Two tbsps. of coconut milk
- One and half tbsp. of fish sauce
- Half tsp. of cayenne pepper
- Two and a half tbsp. of brown sugar
- One-third tsp. of shrimp paste
- Three garlic cloves (minced)
- One chili (minced)

Method:

1. Rinse the shrimps and remove the shells. Cut down the shrimp following the length of the back up to the tail.

2. Add all the listed ingredients in a high power food processor. Blend for making a fine paste.

3. Pour the paste of over the shrimps. Marinate for five minutes.

4. Add the shrimps in a baking tray. Broil the shrimps for four minutes. Add the remaining

marinade over shrimps and broil again for three minutes.

5. Serve immediately.

Thai Crab Cake

Total Prep & Cooking Time: Thirty minutes
Yields: Four servings
Nutrition Facts: Calories: 68.6 | Protein: 5.6g | Carbs:
6.2g | Fat: 2.2g | Fiber: 0.5g

Ingredients

- Eight ounces of crab meat
- Three spring onions (sliced)
- Three lime leaves (thinly sliced)
- One chili (minced)
- One tbsp. of lime juice
- Two tbsps. of fish sauce
- One-fourth tbsp. of oyster sauce
- Three large eggs
- Two tsps. of mayonnaise
- Two cups of panko bread crumbs
- Half tsp. of garlic salt
- One cup of oil

Method:

1. Add crab meat, lime leaves, onions, chili, fish sauce, lime juice, one egg, oyster sauce, half cup of panko bread crumbs, and mayonnaise in a blender. Process the ingredients for two minutes. You can add more bread crumbs if needed.

2. Make cakes from the mixture using your hands. Keep aside.

3. Break the remaining eggs in a bowl. Whisk the eggs.

4. Add bread crumbs and garlic salt in a dish. Mix well.

5. Dip the prepared crab cakes in the whisked eggs and then coat them in the bread crumbs mixture.

6. Heat oil in a pan. Add the crab cakes. Fry for two minutes on each side.

7. Serve hot.

Thai Sticky Meatballs

Total Prep & Cooking Time: Thirty-five minutes
Yields: Six servings
Nutrition Facts: Calories: 330.2 | Protein: 17.6g |
Carbs: 21.3g | Fat: 16.5g | Fiber: 0.9g

Ingredients

For the meatballs:

- One cup of bread crumbs
- One large egg
- One tbsp. of green curry paste
- One tsp. of each
- Ginger paste
- Garlic paste
- One-fourth tsp. of salt
- One and a half tbsp. of fish sauce
- Five-hundred grams of beef (ground)

For the sauce:

- Two tbsps. of each
- Sweet chili sauce
- Soy sauce
- Honey
- One tbsp. of rice vinegar
- Two chilies (chopped)
- Half cup of water
- One tsp. of corn flour

Method:

1. Preheat your oven at two-hundred degrees Celsius.

2. Mix all the listed ingredients for the meatballs except for the beef. Add the ground beef and mix well.

3. Make twenty balls from the beef mixture. Place them on a baking sheet. Bake for twenty-five minutes.

4. Whisk the sauce ingredients in a bowl. Add the sauce to a wok and warm for two minutes.

5. Add the meatballs and toss them in the sauce.

6. Serve hot.

Red Curry Puffs

Total Prep & Cooking Time: Thirty minutes
Yields: Four servings
Nutrition Facts: Calories: 180.6 | Protein: 5.6g |
Carbs: 24.8g | Fat: 6.6g | Fiber: 0.4g

Ingredients

For the filling:

- One medium-sized potato
- One tbsp. of each
- Fish sauce
- Soy sauce
- One tsp. of each
- Red curry paste
- Chili paste
- Four tbsps. of each
- Corn
- Peas

For the wrappers:

- One egg white
- Thirty wonton wrappers
- One tbsp. of each
- Olive oil
- Cornstarch
- Two tbsps. of water

Method:

1. Start by boiling the potato.

2. Combine cornstarch and water in a bowl.

3. Mash the potato and mix it with curry paste, peas, soy sauce, chili paste, and fish sauce. Make a fine paste.

4. Heat your oven and two-hundred degrees Celsius.

5. Take the wonton wrappers and line the borders with the cornstarch mixture.

6. Add one tsp. of the paste in the middle of each wrapper and fold them in a triangle shape.

7. Combine egg white with one tsp. of water. Brush the filled wrappers with the mixture.

8. Bake the puffs in the oven for ten minutes.

9. Serve hot.

Thai Mango Pudding

Total Prep & Cooking Time: Two hours and thirty minutes
Yields: Four servings
Nutrition Facts: Calories: 251.3 | Protein: 4.2g | Carbs: 31.3g | Fat: 14.6g | Fiber: 3.2g

Ingredients

- Two ripe mangoes
- One packet of gelatin
- Half a cup of hot water
- One-third cup of white sugar
- One cup of coconut milk

Method:

1. Scoop out the mango flesh and add it to a blender. Puree the mango flesh.

2. Heat some oil in pan two minutes. Remove the pan from heat. Add the gelatin. Mix well.

3. Add white sugar to the mixture of gelatin.

4. Add the gelatin mixture to the prepared mango puree. Add the coconut milk and combine.

5. Pour the prepared mango mixture into bowls. Refrigerate for two hours.

Thai Crème Caramel

Total Prep & Cooking Time: Thirty-five minutes
Yields: Four servings
Nutrition Facts: Calories: 205.6 | Protein: 5.1g |
Carbs: 26.2g | Fat: 10.3g | Fiber: 0.2g

Ingredients

- One cup of coconut milk
- Two large eggs
- One tbsp. of sugar
- One-fourth tsp. of pandan paste
- One-fourth cup of Thai palm sugar
- One pinch of salt
- One tsp. of coconut oil

Method:

1. Preheat your oven at one-hundred and seventy-five degrees Celsius.

2. Grease four ramekins using oil.

3. Beat the eggs using a fork. Add sugar, salt, pandan paste, and coconut milk. Mix well.

4. Add palm sugar at the bottom of each ramekin.

5. Pour the prepared mixture into the ramekins.

6. Arrange the ramekins on a baking dish. Add some water for covering one-fourth of the ramekins.

7. Bake for thirty minutes.

8. Chill the ramekins for five minutes.

9. Use a sharp knife for running along the inside wall of ramekins.

10. Overturn the loosened ramekins on serving plates.

11. Serve immediately.

Thai-Style Iced Coffee

Total Prep & Cooking Time: One hour and ten minutes
Yields: Four servings
Nutrition Facts: Calories: 110.3 | Protein: 3.2g | Carbs: 16.9g | Fat: 4.1g | Fiber: 0.2g

Ingredients

- Two large cups of brewed coffee
- Six tbsps. of condensed milk
- One-third cup of ice cubes
- One-fourth cup of heavy cream

Method:

1. Pour the coffee in a jug. Add condensed milk. Stir well for mixing. Add a few cubes of ice and refrigerate for one hour.

2. Pour the iced coffee in glasses with ice cubes. Add heavy cream from the top.

Thai Tapioca Pudding

Total Prep & Cooking Time: Thirty minutes
Yields: Four servings
Nutrition Facts: Calories: 310.3 | Protein: 2.1g |
Carbs: 1.3g | Fat: 5.6g | Fiber: 0.3g

Ingredients

- Half cup of tapioca
- Three cups of water
- One-eighth tsp. of salt
- One can of coconut milk
- One mango (sliced)
- Maple syrup (for serving)

Method:

1. Cover tapioca with one and a half cups of water in a bowl. Soak for twenty minutes.

2. Combine salt, tapioca, and two cups of water in a bowl. Boil the mixture and simmer for ten minutes.

3. Let the mixture sit for ten minutes.

4. Refrigerate the mixture for thirty minutes.

5. For serving, scoop out one-fourth cup of tapioca in serving bowls. Add one-third cup of coconut milk. Stir for mixing.

6. Garnish with mango slices and maple syrup.

Mangosteen Clafouti

Total Prep & Cooking Time: One hour and ten minutes
Yields: Six servings
Nutrition Facts: Calories: 165.3 | Protein: 5.6g | Carbs: 23.1g | Fat: 5.6g | Fiber: 0.6g

Ingredients

- Five mangosteen fruit
- Two tbsps. of sugar
- One tsp. of cornstarch
- One-third cup of rice flour
- Four eggs
- One pinch of salt
- One cup of coconut milk
- One-third tsp. of each
- Vanilla extract
- Lemon peel (grated)
- Coconut extract

Method:

1. Preheat your oven at one-hundred and seventy-five degrees Celsius.

2. Grease six ramekins with oil.

3. Use a knife for removing the stem section of the fruits. Remove the skin. Remove the white segments of the fruit.

4. Toss the fruit with one tbsp. of sugar and cornstarch.

5. Arrange the fruit segments at the bottom of the ramekins.

6. Whisk eggs with sugar and salt in a bowl. Add flour and mix well.

7. Add lemon peel, coconut milk, coconut extract, and vanilla extract. Mix well.

8. Pour the mixture into each ramekin.

9. Place the ramekins in a baking dish. Pour two cups of water in the dish.

10. Bake for one hour.

Dragon Fruit Martini

Total Prep & Cooking Time: Twelve minutes
Yields: Two servings
Nutrition Facts: Calories: 121.3 | Protein: 1.1g | Carbs: 10.2g | Fat: 3.2g | Fiber: 0.9g

Ingredients

- One dragon fruit (ripe)
- Half cup of vodka
- One tbsp. of lime juice
- Three tbsps. of white sugar
- Four ice cubes
- One-fourth cup of coconut milk

Method:

1. Scoop out the flesh of the dragon fruit.

2. Add the fruit flesh in a blender. Add the remaining ingredients. Blend for one minute.

3. Serve the chilled martini in glasses and garnish with small pieces of dragon fruit.

Conclusion

Thank you for making it through to the end of *Thai Cuisine*, let's hope it was informative and able to provide you with all of the tools you need to achieve your goals whatever they may be.

Now, all you are required to do is start preparing all the recipes shared in this book. Regardless of your present location, you can now enjoy tasty Thai recipes from your home kitchen. Thai cuisine is very simple, and all it needs is a little effort from your side. Not getting time to visit a Thai restaurant? No need to worry as copycat Thai recipes are here for your rescue. Not sure what to prepare for your guests and friends? Just follow the recipes that I have mentioned in this book, and you are good to go. You can surprise your family members and guests with the authentic flavors of Thai cuisine right from your home kitchen.

In fact, cooking food at home comes with its own set of specialties. You can regulate the use of various ingredients and experiment with the flavors according to your wish. Also, you can discard the use of various types of additives that are used by restaurants. So, what are you waiting for? Pick up your shopping bag and rush to the grocery store to get the Thai cuisine essentials.

If you enjoyed this book, please let me know your thoughts by leaving a short review. Thank you!

"Other books by Arsenio Islas"

Copycat Cookbook: *Japanese Cuisine: 100+ Delicious, Quick and Easy Recipes to Follow to Prepare your Favorite Dishes at the Home Restaurant. Including Cooking Techniques for Beginners*

Copycat Recipes: *Mexican Cuisine 100+ Delicious, Quick and Easy Recipes, Including Cooking Techniques for Beginners, From Appetizers to Desserts*

Copycat Recipes Making: *American Cuisine 100+ Delicious Recipes The Complete Step-By-Step Guide for Making Your Favorite Restaurant Recipes at Home. From Appetizers to Desserts*

Copycat:4 Manuscripts: American Cuisine Japanese Cuisine Thai Cuisine Mexican Cuisine

Lightning Source UK Ltd.
Milton Keynes UK
UKHW021825191120
373696UK00003B/428